"Every page of *The Writer's Advantage* offers remarkable discoveries on the art and craft of writing. Most significantly, Laurie Scheer seems to have cracked the code on why some Hollywood films hit and others completely miss the mark. Her amazing insights and analysis explores not only the form of genres, but their profound function as well — inspiring writers to open their stories to amazing creative possibilities."
— Dara Marks, Hollywood's #1 rated script consultant

"Laurie Scheer's *The Writer's Advantage* is a wonderful handbook for bridging generational gaps in the world of writing and selling your material. That is only one of its attributes. It organizes a way of thinking and educating yourself to write and sell your material. It is filled with entertaining examples and at the end of each chapter is a 'sandbox' full of tools to enhance your understanding of writing and selling material. Laurie has toiled successfully in the minefields of the entertainment business and she knows of what she speaks. The book is really fun and interactive. Can't recommend it highly enough to anyone who is interested in or wants to work in the entertainment field."
— Joan Darling, actress and Emmy and DGA winning director

"Gone are weak scripts and novel manuscripts based on one-dimensional ideas. That's the promise here, and Laurie Scheer delivers. She's cracked the puzzle as to how you make sure you're writing or buying an original idea. *The Writer's Advantage* should be required reading for every writer and executive in the script and novel worlds — as well as all students in MFA and screenwriting programs. This down-to-earth yet authoritative book shows you in masterful steps how to be original — a huge feat. And it delivers by teaching us all how to find the core of a genre's rules or conventions. Every exercise here is a superb gold nugget of storytelling technique. On your book shelf next to Syd Field, Christopher Vogler, Linda Seger, and maybe one or two other teachers who changed the writing industry, you need to add this essential media goddess — Laurie Scheer."
— Christine DeSmet, screenwriting instructor, award-winning screenwriter and mystery series author

"Laurie Scheer takes her years as an industry profession-l combined with her role as an educator, and blends the two in a text that is hon   -ducational. Each chapter includes a Toolkit Sandbox, complete w tions for critical thinking, and exercises to maximize this book truly gives writers an advantage!"
— Wendy Moore, Full Sail University faculty and StayF

"Laurie Scheer's *The Writer's Advantage* is without a
I've come across for writing genre, regardless of medium. With a
media storytelling, Scheer's book is both accessible and also a master class in story development."
— Stefan Blitz, Forces of Geek

"*The Writer's Advantage* forces you to dig a little deeper for the core of an original idea. It gives you the resources to analyze and understand your audience so that you will be better able to deliver a satisfying storytelling experience."
— Tom Farr, Tom Farr Reviews

"The consummate guide to writing, pitching, and finding an audience. Indispensable for all creators."
— Dave Watson, Movies Matter

"I've published many short essays and articles, but the concept of a novel (even chick lit) overwhelmed me. Then came *The Writer's Advantage* — a fun workbook with easy to use tools and techniques. Doing Laurie Scheer's suggested genre research, and answering the questions she poses, has taken the anxiety out of the novel writing process for me. My characters have come to life, and their situations are more timely and amusing thanks to *The Writer's Advantage!*"
— Ellen Nordberg, blogger, *Treading the Twin Tsunami*

"Whether you are creating a novel, film script, web/TV series, memoir, play, game or transmedia project, *The Writer's Advantage* is sure to become your new 'go-to' writing resource! Author Laurie Scheer — aka 'Media Goddess' — deftly guides you to shape, define and embrace your project, giving you the essential tools needed to strengthen and expand your storytelling voice and perspective. Of special note are the invaluable case studies, thought-provoking questions, and results-oriented exercises at the end of each chapter which are designed to jump-start your creative process, no matter what genre you may be pursuing."
— Kathie Fong Yoneda, story consultant, workshop leader, author of *The Script-Selling Game: A Hollywood Insider's Guide to Getting Your Script Sold and Produced (2nd edition)*

"As an agent, I often find that the most promising writers are those who not only create, but know how and why their creations work. *The Writer's Advantage* is a wonderful resource that gets you thinking outside the covers on your way to becoming the author of the future: informed, targeted, and transmedia-savvy."
— Gordon Warnock, founding partner, Foreword Literary

"Laurie Scheer knows what so many writing instructors don't: that understanding how content is consumed, and who is consuming it, is just as crucial as craft. She's given you *The Writer's Advantage*. For God's sake, take it."
— Brad Schreiber, screenwriter, producer, consultant, author, *What Are You Laughing At? How to Write Funny Screenplays, Stories and More*

"Seriously, thank you for writing this book. The exercises were really helpful. The 36 plots — wonderful! The list of websites — great! This book is very clear and not hard to 'get.' This is about knowing the product — your screenplay — and knowing the reasons why it needs to be made. The only way it could be any better is if you could implant a chip in my brain so I can recall all this vital information with a blink of an eye."
— Jane Barbara, writer/producer, Testa Dura Media/Women in Film & Video-DC Vice President, Chair, ScriptDC

"Only someone with the depth and breadth of Laurie Scheer's first-hand experience could create such an indispensable resource for all aspiring writers. *The Writer's Advantage* is chock-full of effective tools, step-by-step instruction, and industry insights that will take your labor of love from concept, to pitch, to presentation, to a produced project. Eagerly read, successfully followed, and highly recommended."
— Josie Brown, author, *The Housewife Assassin's Handbook* series, and *Totlandia* series

"To paraphrase Laurie Scheer's 'Three Questions for Writers': *Why make this book?* To enlighten and candidly assist writers to understand the secrets that have been locked behind closed story development doors forever and how to navigate the road to success. The author has provided a toolbox and the way to 'take control of your writing destiny,' with enormous first-hand information and understanding. *Why make this book now?* Because it's needed! It's been missing for years. This book is certain to become a coveted document translated into many languages for writers all over the world. The myriad of tools inside the toolbox is destined for the writer's computer for instant ready reference. *The Writer's Advantage* sets the reader on the way to becoming their 'own private development department.' *Who cares about this book?* Everybody who is a writer or desires to become a writer. The secrets are out of the box, written by a person who has been through the doors and maneuvered through the trenches. The only thing missing from this book is what to wear on the day of your meeting and the shortest distance from your home or office to the place of your meeting so that you're a few minutes early."
— Cynthia Comsky, Chair of PLAYdate at the Ebell of Los Angeles, Ebell Playwright Prize, 2nd Wednesdays at the Ebell and Co-Chair of Ebell Social Services Committee; former TV executive producer

"Brings great value to book authors in advising them to view their writing through the lens of film and TV trends, in particular to (1) know their genre, including its history and evolution; (2) understand their particular dramatic situation, and (3) identify and write for their audience, which as a rule all have shortening attention spans, and are consuming content across multiple platforms."
— April Eberhardt, literary change agent/owner, April Eberhardt Literary

"If you're a serious writer, be it film, TV, web, or books, you must constantly take action to move your career forward. By knowing your genre inside and out you are well on your way to becoming a successful writer. Without knowledge and understanding of your genre you risk a fate of not being taken seriously. Laurie Scheer offers a comprehensive study and the tools you need to make your story appeal to the audience you are seeking. She will teach you how to make your writing marketable and profitable. Read this book before you write yours."
— Forris Day Jr., writer/reviewer for *ScaredStiffReviews.com* and *Scriptmag.com*

"Separating the wheat from the chaff, *The Writer's Advantage* is my new go-to resource. More than a toolkit for writers, it's a treasure trove of valuable insights from a seasoned professional. The case studies, questions, and exercises at the end of each chapter are invaluable! They challenged me to remove potentially rose-colored glasses and see (really see!) my work as an unbiased observer. As a writer I will continue to use *The Writer's Advantage* as a fulcrum to raise my work to a higher level and prepare it for successful placement in the marketplace."
— Laurie Buchanan, PhD, transformational life coach

"There's a proliferation of interchangeable screenwriting guides on the market, but Laurie Scheer's *The Writer's Advantage* is wholly unique. As its title proclaims, it's not just a 'how-to,' but a fundamental approach to navigating today's ever-changing media landscape. It's everything writers aren't thinking about — but should be."
— Greg Lessans, producer, screenwriter, film executive

"The perfect book for any writer who's willing to do the work. And trust me, you'll work. There are no shortcuts in *The Writer's Advantage*. What you *will* find is a road map to being the best writer you can be. The importance of genre knowledge has never been as eloquently stated or as deeply investigated as it is here. I write across multiple mediums and I found myself applying some of these tools to all of them. I only wish I'd had this book years ago when I first started putting pen to paper."
— Steve Belanger, writer, actor, podcast host

"In Hollywood as well as in all media, everything begins with writing. Seems everybody thinks they can be a writer. To truly be a 'writer' you must understand the craft. In *The Writing's Advantage*, Laurie Scheer helps the aspiring writer to develop their style, understand the marketplace, and hopefully bring the work to a receptive audience. Scheer provides the coaching and cheerleading each writer needs. She shares so many elements and techniques to enhance one's efforts. There are real-world examples to help each writer succeed. If you want to make writing your livelihood, you need to use this book and you must refer to it over and over."
— Laurence L. Levin, photographer and educator

"If you are a writer and you're writing the next great screenplay or novel, make sure you have a copy of *The Writer's Advantage* in hand. You'll want to refer to it *before* you begin your writing, *during,* and especially afterwards, when you begin your pitching and marketing process. As a manager and producer, I am letting all of my clients know about this very important volume of work. You'll find the information is invaluable and evergreen and, more importantly, your projects will have the necessary elements to aid in setting up your project and making it marketable."
— Marilyn R. Atlas, literary and talent manager, producer, *Real Women Have Curves,*
  Choking Game

"Laurie's book completely sets the record straight with what is happening in present day media outlets. Before reading, I was feeling overwhelmed and confused, but she broke it down into understandable overviews... plus, I loved the end-of-chapter bullet points and checklists. It drives it all home."
— Kendra Cunningham, comic, creator of *Blonde Logic* and *lonelygirl48*

"The lessons Laurie Scheer taught me still resound years later. Her mentorship, practical advice, and wisdom about all things 'story' have been invaluable to my success as a writer, and this book is another amazing tool she's given us to navigate the storyscape."
— Dominique Ferrari, screenwriter, currently in production with a "Black List" script

"In a world filled with an overabundance of tips, tricks, and tools of every kind, never has a book been so clear and straight to the point than *The Writer's Advantage*. Scheer lays everything out in a concise yet engaging fashion that is relatable and easy to follow. The chapter-end exercises are essential in helping you write your best screenplay yet. How to sell your project is also discussed, which, in today's conglomerated world, can feel like an impossible task. Thank you Laurie Scheer for providing us with a tool that is essential in creating the greatest films of our future."
— Lauren Zink, US Advice Network Manager at VICE Media, Inc.

The Writer's
ADVANTAGE

A TOOLKIT FOR MASTERING YOUR GENRE
LAURIE SCHEER

．
．

MICHAEL WIESE PRODUCTIONS

Published by Michael Wiese Productions
12400 Ventura Blvd. #1111
Studio City, CA 91604
(818) 379-8799, (818) 986-3408 (FAX)
mw@mwp.com
www.mwp.com

Cover design by Johnny Ink. www.johnnyink.com
Interior design by William Morosi
Printed by McNaughton & Gunn

Manufactured in the United States of America
Copyright 2014 by Laurie Scheer

Library of Congress Cataloging-in-Publication Data

Scheer, Laurie.
  The writer's advantage : a toolkit for mastering your genre / Laurie Scheer.
      pages cm
  Includes bibliographical references.
  ISBN 978-1-61593-198-9
  1. Television authorship. 2. Motion picture authorship. 3. Mass media--Authorship. I. Title.
  PN1992.7.S36 2014
  808.06'6791--dc23

                          2014001701

Printed on Recycled Stock

TABLE OF CONTENTS

SECTION TWO
ARMING YOURSELF

CHAPTER 11
CHECKLISTING YOUR AUTHENTIC MATERIAL 109

SECTION THREE
GETTING YOUR WORK OUT INTO THE WORLD

CHAPTER 12
DEFENDING YOUR WORK 121

CHAPTER 13
WHAT MASTERING YOUR GENRE CAN DO FOR YOU 129

This book is dedicated to my holy trinity of mentors:

Dr. James T. Tiedge, Norma Herron, and Delle Chatman.

And also to Syd Field, everyone's first screenplay mentor.

ACKNOWLEDG-MENTS

Kathie Fong Yoneda has believed in this book since its inception and I thank her for sharing the proposal with Ken Lee and Michael Wiese and for believing in me and my work. How refreshing it was that Ken understood the basic essence of my idea and soon he and Michael gave me a green light to move forward. I am honored to be a part of the family.

So many amazing individuals have provided their support and I have been blessed with their grace and assistance during the writing of this book. I thank the great, wise sage Christopher Vogler — without you all writers aspiring to tell their stories would be lost, including myself. You have been a guiding light for me for more than two decades. Ellen Nordberg, a true friend, I thank you for showing up in my class at U-of-C in the mid-'90s and never — not even for a second — failing to be one of my life's spiritual advisors ever since. Judy Molland, you have always been there for me and most especially when we were in DC — gracias and merci! Josie Brown, you inspire me daily as you are truly the hardest working author I know, and Dale Kushner, thank you for your ultramarine sparks — how would I have ever lived without them?

Christine DeSmet, thank you for the always beautiful goddess sunbeams, and thanks Laura Kahl, you know so well how to be a swan — I'm still learning how to master that one.

To Brad Schrieber, thank you. I am honored to call you friend. Film pixie Killian Heilsberg, thank you, we only children rock! Gregory Johnson, my soulmate, I love you, thank you, and Wayne Christensen and Nikko for the use of The Fort and for your love — it is wonderful, it sure is, it sure is.

I am appreciative of the folks who believe in me year after year and who have let me share this material with students and conference attendees. Most especially my thanks to Melissa Houghton and Jane Barbara of WIFV DC. Your support means so much. Additionally, thanks to Kristin Oakley and her In Print Writers' Group, you gave me great feedback and incentive to continue onward. Also eternal thanks to the attendees of my Write By The Lake Retreat session, Summer 2013, I treasure your support and my precious copy of *Zen and the Art of Motorcycle Maintenance*.

To my mother and father, thank you for your love and for teaching me the practical factors of life and for letting me watch all the television I ever wanted to.

And finally, hugs and smiles (in that order) to Eric Martinot for your integrity, timing, and continuous support the second time around. Thanks for making sure we achieved our New Years' Intentions.

And thank you to my students — past, present, and future — who continue to teach me so much more than I could have ever imagined.

Laurie Scheer
December, 2013

FOREWORD

BY

CHRISTOPHER
VOGLER

I like a book that agrees with me. I like it when the author says what I believe, only in better words and with more convincing evidence. I also like a book that tells me things I didn't know, or that identifies patterns I hadn't fully understood before. *The Writer's Advantage* does both. In its pages I found confirmation of things I've observed and suspected about the way entertainment is made, and I also found lucid explanations of what is happening in the rapidly changing media universe. In fact, I really had little idea what that universe, currently called "transmedia," might actually be. Now I think I do, thanks to the author's clarity and depth of informed knowledge on the subject. Further, the author's intention is to provide you with practical techniques for avoiding the current plague of repetitive, predictable, bombastic, and mindlessly overproduced sequels and remakes. She can even guide you beyond that, to create something totally new for a totally new storytelling environment.

This book has changed my consciousness about the present moment in the history of story-based entertainment. I was aware something was different. Who could fail to notice that stories in conventional Hollywood movies and network television have become more derivative and unwilling to take risks, while entertainment made for cable and many new outlets seems fresher and more authentic? However, the author pinpoints the exact moment in time when that began to happen, using a technique of analysis very similar to my own, which is to look at culture trends with an awareness of chronology and context. In other words, examine the evolution of an idea, a literary property, a story technique or a genre year by year, tracing that development from its earliest beginnings, and closely observing how it altered because of audience reactions and everything else that was going on in the ever-changing jet stream of culture. Know the field you are studying in depth, taking into account all the other developments in the surrounding field of entertainment and society. She offers this approach, part of "The Writer's Advantage," as a practical tool for making your work an exciting and novel expansion of worn-out genres, or perhaps even for creating entirely new forms of entertainment.

The author is a seasoned observer of the story development machinery, and correctly points out its flaws and weaknesses. One of these is what she calls a "fanboy" tendency in screen-writers, directors, and story executives. Too often, those controlling media these days were raised upon works of recent years that were already derivative of literature and movies of the past. Fanboys and fangirls create works that are purposely derivative, based on superficial knowledge and understanding of the genres in which they dare to tread. When I was a development executive, I used to call these lazy-minded professionals "skimmers" and "magpies." They loved to dabble in genres, or loot and pillage from classic works of literature and cinema to create slapdash remakes, but like magpies they were attracted only to the shiniest and most superficial aspects of the genres and works, ignoring or completely missing the glowing radioactive essence of those beloved forms. All they could bring to the classic designs was greater volume, more extreme violence or outrageous episodes, cruder language, hokier and more unrealistic behavior. And often they seemed to deliberately stomp on the true hearts of these genres, subverting them or belittling the very things that made them charming and magical in the first place. Fortunately, the author offers realistic remedies for this fanboy tendency, by urging writers to develop much deeper and broader understanding of the genres in which they hope to make a contribution.

In these pages I read with approval the author's critique of what has been called "Chaos Cinema," movies in which there is a high proportion of visually confusing destruction and violence, typically the entire last quarter or third of the experience. As the author says it, "Unintelligible sensory overload abides in this arena." The signal-to-noise ratio is set so that there is a lot of noise and very little signal; i.e., very little emotional content or advancement of the grand design of the story. So often these days the actual story seems to stop, parked on a siding somewhere, while the filmmakers indulge themselves in an orgy of flying metal, in which what little dialogue there may be is impossible to understand, and I am not entirely sure if what just spun across the screen is the torn-off wheel of a machine or the hero's severed head. To me the unintelligibility is a great crime against the economy and clarity of cinema. I stand here with Lord Raglan, the English aristocrat who wrote a definitive study of heroes in legend and folklore. One of his rules was: "Everything that is said and done upon the stage must be intelligible to the audience."

While using rational tools of analysis, the author never loses sight of a quality she calls "wonderment," an essential element in her view for creating unique new expressions in modern media. Too often in place of true wonderment we find an effort to overwhelm the viewer with digitally-rendered eye candy, with special effects that are no longer special. Simple magic is sometimes the best. Little illusions performed right on the stage, or the small enchantment of an actor creating a word picture or an emotional breakthrough, can still outweigh the impact of an 89-million-dollar post-production budget.

Among the many gems of wisdom found here, gleaned from a career of close observation and hard-won experience, is the author's insistence that it's a long game, writing for media and working with genres. Sometimes, when you get rejected because your idea seems untimely, it's just because you're ahead of your time. Projects don't always find their ideal moment in history right away, and may need to be stored away somewhere, carefully, until the time-waves of the zeitgeist coincide to make that project feel fresh and new or simply perfect for that moment in the culture. I can attest that many times I've seen story concepts shouted down or laughed out of the room because they seemed hopelessly out-of-date, only to find them returning a decade or so later as if they had just been minted to answer a need of the moment. Of course, like old fashions hanging in your closet, they may have to be re-tailored a bit or reconceived to emphasize the qualities that have been missing from the media environment.

One of the author's most useful contributions may be pinpointing the effect she calls "fragmentation" — the breaking up of audiences and means of delivering the story experience. Where not so long ago there were a few media outlets dispensing movies, TV shows, and books to a general audience at regular intervals, there is now a shattered landscape in which increasingly balkanized shards of audience consume fragments of entertainment almost randomly. She sees this as a challenge and an opportunity, rather than as a problem, and encourages genre writers to assume a position of mastery, knowing their chosen field of storytelling in great depth and breadth, understanding its history and evolution in view of chronology and context. Instead of getting lost in the web of random connections, she counsels genre writers to remember the tools that have always served storytellers well — linear thinking as well as awareness of cycles and webs, careful analysis as well as fanboy enthusiasm, and genuine understanding of the essential heart that beats in every genre. She points to a high road for genre-loving writers, in which they can not only participate in the forms they admire, but also make fresh contributions that no one has ever imagined, and even spin out completely new genres and styles that others will have the fun of exploring and expanding one day. Enter her world with a sense of wonderment, and you will be rewarded.

Christopher Vogler is author of *The Writer's Journey*, co-author of *Memo From the Story Department*, and a former Fox development executive.

HOW TO USE THIS BOOK

Following in the tradition of Syd Field's *Screenplay* books and *A Writer's Journey* by Christopher Vogler, *The Writer's Advantage: A Toolkit for Mastering Your Genre* is the next step for every type of writer. From time to time, writers need a contemporaneous manual to assist them with developing and writing their material and — just as important — preparing that material for the marketplace. Just as Syd Field provided the bare bones information needed to write an effective script in the late '70s, and as Christopher Vogler outlined mythic structure as a way for writers to organize their storylines and characters in the mid-'90s, this book assists writers traverse the 21st century transmedia universe — a marketplace that includes all platforms: print, theatrical distribution, broadcast and cable networks, web channels and websites (including internet radio and podcasts). You'll learn about the tools you'll need to navigate through the waters of creating authentic and competitive ideas, avoiding plagiarism, and assuring that your ideas find an audience in this complicated and vast fluctuating marketplace — all giving you what I call "The Writer's Advantage."

THE BOOK'S REASON FOR BEING

We have arrived at a time when mass media is not so "mass" any longer. With so many ways to access and enjoy information and entertainment, the multitasking consumer only has time to comprehend a fraction of a text. It is rare that we consume a book or movie or television series in its entirety, and if we do we are usually marathon reading or binge watching texts. This leads to a great deal of miscommunication among consumers who may say "Yeah, sure, I know the show *Mad Men*" within a conversation, but they may have only watched it once or twice. Or, "I saw the latest *Iron Man* movie," however, during the movie, they texted with their about-to-be-ex-girlfriend through-out the second half of the film, meanwhile losing elements of the storyline overall. We now exist in a culture of missed opportunities due to distractions, multitasking, and the conve-nience of advancing technology. Awareness of this is important because consumers are confused and overloaded — they think they may know of a text from popular culture, but they prob-ably know very little about that text, and writers dangerously set out to write within their genre having only a fraction of the knowledge of that genre before and while they are writing their work. Writers then go out into the world naively selling medio-cre and non-authentic material. In addition, those who choose material to be published and produced (development depart-ment execs, editors, producers) are also following along these lines and the result is what we currently see on the best-selling lists, at the box office, and on TV, and that is a preponderance of sequels, prequels, remakes, and reboots. Where are the original ideas?

What we have is a group of writers and publishing/entertain-ment execs who are mere followers. We need innovative writers who arm themselves with information, know complete texts within their genre, and eventually find their own voice and their own authentic texts. We need story innovators.

WHAT THIS BOOK CAN DO FOR YOU

Half of the information in this book assists you in mastering your genre and the other half is about what that mastering can do for you.

This book assists you —

1. as you begin a new writing project.
2. while you are writing a project.
3. when you feel your text just isn't ready or perfect.
4. when you have been shopping your material and receiving consistent rejections.

In this book, the term "texts" is used to describe material any given writer may be writing. When the term "texts" is used, I could be referring to any (or all) of the following types of writing:

- manuscripts for novels and novellas
- manuscripts for short story and poetry anthologies
- manuscripts for flash and fan fiction
- memoirs
- nonfiction manuscripts
- screenplays for feature-length and short theatrical movies
- screenplays for movies made for television
- screenplays and bibles for television series
- screenplays for web series

Ideally, it is advantageous to read the book in its entirety before you begin writing for the transmedia marketplace because of the information you'll discover through research and your new awareness of the overall scope of the market.

Should you feel that you only want to zero in on improving a project that is already started, then utilizing the information in the first two sections of the book — KNOW WHAT HAS BEEN DONE BEFORE and ARMING YOURSELF — will give you the necessary background information needed to assist you in reworking what you have completed so far. If you have been out shopping your work and receiving rejection after rejection, then begin with the final section GETTING YOUR WORK OUT INTO THE WORLD, make your adjustments in keeping with the information therein, and go back out into the marketplace.

Here are some specific ways to best utilize the material in this book:

1. If you're a first-time writer, Sections One and Two, Chapters 1 through 11 are best for you to read to understand this complex marketplace of transmedia entertainment.

2. If you've had some success with short stories or an indie film, but you are stuck on how to keep the momentum going and you want to complete a full-fledged book/novel or script, it would be advantageous for you to read Section Two, Chapters 5 through 11.

3. If you are on deadline and must deliver a draft yesterday, however you're not sure how to make sure your manuscript/script is in tip-top shape, then access Chapters 8, 9, and 10 to zero in on the specific background of your genre.

4. If you want to adapt your own work via a manuscript or script, Chapter 8 is for you — I'd suggest reading that chapter twice and playing with the Toolkit Sandbox items.

5. If you have had difficulty pitching your project and you've received little interest from potential buyers, then Section Three, Chapters 12, 13, and 14 are for you.

6. If you are a veteran writer looking to identify new horizons for your genre and what your genre will look like 1 to 3 years out,

Chapters 8, 9, and 10 are certain to provide insight and fuel for your fire.

7. If you think your work is not ready, yet you're not certain why that may be, be sure to read Chapter 12 and learn how to defend your work.

The information available within this book can be applied to your current project and future writing projects again and again. If you write within a specific genre and have established your brand within that genre, then you can continue to build upon the research you gather for each project you are composing — even if you want to produce a hybrid or sub-genre within genres, or switch to a new genre. The book is an evergreen manual to be used throughout your writing career.

BEING A FANBOY VS. BEING A FAN OF MEDIA

The transmedia landscape did not exist when I was coming up in the entertainment industry and academia. It is because of my experience of working within the traditional hallways of a broadcast network and processing media in a pre-fragmented world that I am able to present this method of writing to you. If I hadn't been taught in the old-school ways, I would not be able to share this insight with you. That said, I am not so much a fan of any of the specific genres discussed in this book as I am a fan of the way these genres and media in general has been and continues to be delivered and consumed. I'm not the fanboy (those dedicated individuals who are fanatic fans of say, a certain franchise like *Star Wars* or the *Twilight* series), but I am the coach for fanboys everywhere as they write and distribute their material via 21st century transmedia platforms. You are no longer just writing a stand-alone novel or feature film. Within a transmedia marketplace your idea can be repurposed, rebroadcast, and/or refurbished for each of the various transmedia platforms. You need to think beyond the original incarnation of your project and the sooner you realize this, the easier it is going to be for you to be profitable within this arena.

UNIQUELY QUALIFIED

When I arrived in Hollywood in the early '80s I did not have a specific goal, I only knew that I wanted to be involved in the behind-the-scenes goings-on of the entertainment industry. When I took my first job as an assistant in the Dramatic Development department at ABC in Century City, I didn't even know what "Dramatic Development" meant.

I learned quickly and I embraced skills that have benefitted me throughout my entire career, skills that have adapted well throughout the changes in culture and technology and followed me as I added academic experience on to my industry credits. It seems that I was at the right place, right time at many points in my career, such as:

- From Dramatic Development at ABC, I moved to ABC Motion Pictures, a unique production company that was a branch of a broadcast network.
- A year after joining Viacom Enterprises, Viacom mogul Sumner Redstone acquired MTV, Showtime, Nickelodeon, VH-1 and Ha! (a precursor to Comedy Central), and so there I was acquiring content (known as "material" at the time) for all of these cable networks.
- From there I worked my way up the ladder to Vice President of a cable network — a new, emerging channel called Romance Classics. The network would be renamed as WE: Women's Entertainment.
- Within my academic career, I have also found myself at the beginning of new ventures. I was called upon to co-develop the broadcasting curriculum at a digital academic start-up

in Chicago, and completed the project on deadline and with much success.

- My most recent "first" has been to serve as managing editor of the newly established annual literary journal, the *Midwest Prairie Review*, for a Midwest writing community.

So, from TV networks to film acquisition, to digital academies and literary journals, the basic development skills of identifying strong characters, solid storylines, and meaningful, believable dialogue, along with commercial appeal that would resonate to many — all the elements that I learned in those first few months on my first Hollywood desk — have now been utilized throughout the past three decades and continue to be used daily. I feel I am uniquely qualified to guide you on your writing journey as you master your genre.

TOOLKIT SANDBOX

This book's discussions and exercises are designed for you to have fun with your material and the research you'll conduct. Each chapter ending provides you with a TOOLKIT SANDBOX filled with items to pique your imagination. The minute you are working on a project and you are not having fun you should stop right there and ask why. By reading about these examples, answering the questions, and doing the exercises, you'll develop skills to write authentic texts.

In each chapter within the first two sections you'll find CASE STUDIES that illustrate the subject of that chapter in depth. Next, you'll find the section QUESTIONING WITH THE WRITER'S ADVANTAGE. Answer these questions after you have read and processed each chapter. They are designed to walk you through the material to ensure that you are addressing all the concepts. They are also present so you can have a little fun with the subject matter on hand. And finally, you'll see a chapter EXERCISE. These exercises are designed to assist you in your own unique understanding of the concepts discussed as you apply these concepts to your writing and your writing life.

Take control of your writing destiny — beginning now!

TO BEGIN

As you read these first chapters, here are some general questions you should be asking:

1. Do you know the genre in which you wish to work?
2. Do you know your story?
3. Do you know (in general) what your material will bring to the marketplace?

These questions are addressed at length and in detail within the upcoming chapters. For now, just let the answers to these questions simmer in your mind. Then state your genre, write out a basic one- or two-sentence description of your story (this will later be perfected as your "logline"), and most importantly, write your mission statement in regard to the material you are writing.

In other words, state why you want to bring this idea into the world.

Welcome to *The Writer's Advantage*. Let's move onward toward creating original and authentic texts for the 21st century marketplace!

SECTION ONE

KNOW WHAT HAS BEEN DONE BEFORE

CHAPTER 1

A BRIEF INQUIRY INTO MASS AND NOT-SO-MASS MEDIA

To begin to understand learning how to write with The Writer's Advantage, let's start with a brief discussion about "mass communication," aka "mass media." The "mass" part of mass media has changed, and what we once knew as "mass" media has become a collection of niche media with many more options available to consumers. In the 21st century there exists a very different mass media — so different that it's really now a "not-so-mass" media.

MEDIA CONSUMPTION

We live in a transmedia universe, meaning we all have opportunities to view content on various levels and screens — and all at one time. I can be watching TV on an actual television set or within my computer screen while texting, listening to music, and composing/editing my own movie at the same time. At any given time we have at our fingertips a multitude of instant media options. This is the environment you are writing within and for. You are vying for attention among humans with short attention spans — a hefty and lofty assignment for sure. How do you get their eyeballs to watch your material? How do you invite the gazes of potentially important consumers amidst all of the participating content competition? I believe that it is important to briefly take a look at where media has been to understand how to write for the transmedia marketplace now. We'll look at a brief analysis of how different media have been distributed so far.

MOVIES

Every form of media has its own unique history. The movie industry began at the end of the 19th century with shorts, silent films, and newsreels before it found its stride and full-length feature films were produced.

If you wanted to see a movie in the '50s you went to your local movie palace, usually a grandiose theater located in the central neighborhood of a metropolitan area. If it was a major city, there would be two or three movie theaters. New titles appeared once a week, making for a limited selection, but still, audiences flocked to each new release. The population had one, maybe two selections to choose from, making it easy to discuss the movie afterwards as there was very little competition. This was clearly an unfragmented scenario leading to a good amount of the public viewing the same movies at relatively the same time throughout the early part of the 20th century through to the late '70s/early '80s, when multiplex theater centers first appeared on the scene. By "unfragmented" I mean that the consumers had very limited options.

Today we have multiplex theater centers with 20+ screens located in various parts of any given town along with the ability to view a movie on television via broadcast and cable networks and through Netflix, Amazon, and other web outlets. We can also DVR and download movies at any time and purchase them for our own viewing pleasure. It would be very difficult to have to wait an entire week to see a new movie and then have no choice in regard to the type of movie that might be. We are now a fragmented audience — broken off and separated from other consumers.

TELEVISION

The television industry began in the middle of the 20th century and — following the formatting of radio programming before it — offered fifteen-minute, half-hour, and hour programs usually sponsored for the entire length of the show by one sponsor. It was not until the advertising industry and the broadcast networks began their marriage of approximately four to six ads per half hour/hour that the industry found the operating pattern that we know today. That programming schedule found its way to basic cable networks when they came on the scene in the '80s. The premium cable networks (HBO, Showtime) found they could operate quite well on subscriber monies alone and did not need advertising to interrupt their content.

Within the television industry, there were four commercial networks born in the late 1940s: NBC, CBS, ABC — all off-shoots of established radio companies — and the DuMont Network, the first television-only network. Aside from theatrical movie releases, audiences now had a choice of drama, comedy, variety, news, documentary, talk and game shows to watch at home... and still the audience was unfragmented.

UNFRAGMENTED AUDIENCES

One of the best examples of an unfragmented society watching an event on television is the reporting of President John F. Kennedy's assassination in November, 1963. The footage from newsman Walter Cronkite's teary-eyed delivery of the fatal information that day has become legendary within the history of television. There would be a much happier event just three months later — on February 9, 1964 — that would bring nearly the entire U.S. viewing population together: the arrival of the Beatles in America and their performance on *The Ed Sullivan Show* (1948–1971).

Here is one of the quintessential examples of audience unfragmentation. Over half of the entire American viewing public watched the Beatles that evening. CBS had the majority of the nation's eyeballs and, to this day, those who experienced that event will talk about it as if it were a mythic appearance. The basic contextual meaning of what the Beatles were about was immediately understood. A new generation embraced them, the older generation didn't understand them — but both generations knew who John, Paul, George, and Ringo were.

LIMITED AMOUNT OF TEXTS

This type of programming — where the majority of viewers can recall where they were at the moment it happened — continues through the Golden Age of Television programming [*I Love Lucy* (1951-57), *The Andy Griffith Show* (1960-68), *The Twilight Zone* (1959-64), etc.] and with all of the NASA liftoffs at that time. The finite television network universe had its run until the early '80s and the advent of basic cable programming. Until the early '80s there is only a limited amount of texts for writers to comprehend, write about, spin off of and parody. *The Carol Burnett Show* (1967–78), a well-loved variety hour, would often parody famous films such as *Gone With The Wind* (1939) and popular soap operas and disaster movies of the time. The reason Burnett's parody style was so successful was because the audience had collectively viewed and knew well the original content being parodied. It is nearly impossible for an audience to understand a parody unless they know the original text. This is the secret of the success of *Saturday Night Live* (1975–present), as the show exists purely to parody current series, events, and personalities. The point here is that because of the limited viewing audience, it was fairly easy for writers to find fodder to write about. These limited choices begin to end in the early '80s with the birth of basic cable programming.

THE CABLE REVOLUTION

August 1, 1981, is considered by many to be the birth of basic cable. The first video aired on MTV, The Buggles' "Video Killed the Radio Star," began the cable revolution and soon after nearly a hundred new networks were available to view and purchase by American households. Sure, networks like CNN, Lifetime, and HBO existed in the '70s, but they didn't have the distribution power then. When cable providers such as Time Warner, Cablevision, and Cox Communication, to name a few (depending on where you were located in the country), came into power, that is when the American public had a much larger menu of entertainment options from which to choose.

FRAGMENTED VIEWERSHIP

The fragmentation of viewers begins here. Now you no longer have a large amount of viewers going out to movie theaters and watching the same movie, watching the same network at the same time, or even watching in real-time (the time the series is scheduled on the network's programming schedule) because audiences began taping programming (via video cassette recorders) to watch when it was convenient for them personally. This shift made it more difficult for writers of movies and television/cable shows to relate to all viewers. Soon, a 500-network universe is available to American viewers. The fraction of viewers watching one event/series/network becomes smaller and smaller. With the expanding popularity of personal computers and the "world wide web" in the early to mid '90s, the attention span of a typical content viewer becomes even more fragmented due to the many options available at any time.

WEB CHANNELS

Along with the dawn of the new century, all basic and premium cable networks have ancillary content available on their websites. An example of this might be additional interactive content for children who enjoy the viewing of *Dora the Explorer* (2000–present) on Nickelodeon and then want to visit the website for more information about that episode, and in some cases watch additional episodes of the show. Likewise for all of the lifestyle programs such as house hunting and remodeling homes on a network like HGTV. Their website would soon include video vignettes regarding household projects, the same for The Food Network, etc.

When YouTube appears on the scene in 2005, the birth of consumer-created content begins. Web sensations such as *Fred* (2006) and web channels like *Funny Or Die* (2007) soon follow. The opportunities for writers and creators of content now seem endless, as are the viewing choices for consumers.

SO MANY OPTIONS, SO LITTLE TIME

Today, video gaming, IMING, texting, emailing, gaming, etc., all co-exist. Additionally, with the birth of social networking sites, the amount of people watching/consuming a piece of content from the same resource at the same time becomes even more and more fragmented. Perhaps one of the only events in more recent times that resonated in the way those did in the '60s are the terrorist acts of September 11, 2001. Here is an anomaly in the 21st century — an event that happened that stopped the world. You will always remember where you were and what you were doing when you heard about New York City's World Trade Center being attacked and destroyed. Remember, though, that even at that time viewers had a multitude of television and internet resources through which to get information.

A MENTION ABOUT THE PUBLISHING INDUSTRY

During these decades of change regarding the visual media industries, publishing remained intact. Books of all types would be published in hardcover and then, after a short window of time, released in more affordable paperback versions, prolonging their popularity.

Not much change is seen in publishing until electronic readers appear on the scene in 2004 and consumers find a new way of reading their favorite texts. By the beginning of the second decade of the 21st century, e-books become hefty competition for standard publishing. At the same time, individual authors begin self-publishing and distributing content via the internet. And not long after that, "blogging" is born.

CONTENT IS KING

In all of the types of media we've studied, content is king and has remained king throughout these many decades of changes in distribution and technology. In each type of media, writers are still necessary. None of these industries could survive without writers.

So how do you, the writer, get a handle on this fragmentation? These shorter-than-short attention spans? These multitasking consumers? We'll explore this in the next chapter to learn how to arm ourselves in this fragmented world.

TOOLKIT SANDBOX

A Wizard, Some Questions, and a Mysterious Millionaire

CASE STUDY: THE MAN BEHIND THE CURTAIN AND THE CLASSIC AMERICAN TEXT

Author L. Frank Baum would be astonished today if he knew what has become of his 1900 novel *The Wonderful Wizard of Oz*. During his lifetime he did know that children adored the book, as they wrote him letters asking for more. He obliged them, and in 1904 he wrote the first sequel, with many others to follow — written by himself and by authors designated by his publisher after Baum's death in 1919. An original *Oz* book was published yearly between 1913 and 1942.

And while the books were indeed popular, it is the film version entitled *The Wizard of Oz* (1939), featuring Judy Garland and now-iconic characters and musical numbers, that is imbedded in the psyche of every American (and admirers worldwide) alive during and since that time.

Perhaps it is because this film had the advantage of being shown consistently on network television since 1956 that the content of the books and film remain forever a part of popular culture. This was unusual, as most theatrical movies would be shown nationally on television only once or twice after being released in theaters, and then scheduled late at night or on weekends by regional affiliates. This was not the case with *The Wizard of Oz*, which was broadcast annually and highly advertised as a special event. These broadcast telecasts continued until 1999, at which time the film went to cable and broadcast showings became more frequent.

All of which has resulted in the production of *Oz*-related content in nearly all mediums over the years, including:

The Wiz (1974) — Broadway stage musical that won seven Tony Awards.

The Wiz (1978) — movie adaptation of the Broadway musical starring Michael Jackson and Diana Ross.

The Wizard of Oz (1982) — a Japanese anime feature film.

Return to Oz (1982) — a darker adaptation of *Oz* sequel novels.

Wicked: The Life and Times of the Wicked Witch of the West (1995), a novel by Gregory Maquire that spawns a series of additional books entitled *Son of a Witch* (2005), *A Lion Among Men* (2008), *Out of Oz* (2011).

Wicked (2003) — Broadway stage musical adaptation of Maquire's novel.

The Muppets' Wizard of Oz (2005) — TV movie.

Tin Man (2007) — television miniseries produced for the Syfy channel playing up the sci-fi/fantasy elements of the story.

The Wizard of Oz (2011) — London stage musical composed by Andrew Lloyd Webber.

Oz the Great and Powerful (2013) — movie prequel starring James Franco, telling the story of the wizard's arrival in Oz.

This is by no means a complete list, however it is a list that illustrates how a single basic storyline can be transferred to different genres and released in different versions and venues within a transmedia universe. This content, whether consumed as a book, a film, a film viewed on television, as a musical, or as a prequel in print and film, continues to stand the test of time. *Oz* resonates again and again to generation after generation — all based on a yearly television broadcast of a film that nearly everyone grew up watching.

Additionally, more versions of this original text are planned — a 3D animated film, NBC and CBS are developing series, Syfy has another miniseries in the works, and the 75th anniversary of the original 1939 film may see a re-release in 3D in 2014. Why all this interest in a novel that first appeared over a century ago? That's a good question. This is content that resonates to audiences on a universally human level and has been perpetuated from generation to generation due to its accessibility. As we continue to look at ways to do research in this book we will see that a text like this is very important to observe, as there is something within the text that strikes a nerve with writers and creators and with audiences over and over throughout the decades. Each generation wants to put their mark on these iconic characters and this story about how "there's no place like home," and each generation offers up a new spin, a fresh look at the content. In essence, by observing the history of *The Wonderful Wizard of Oz*, one can clearly see how each version is authentic. Whether the version explores prequel subject matter or injects music or dance or animation, each version is unique in its own way.

QUESTIONING WITH THE WRITER'S ADVANTAGE

1. If you could see only one movie in a theater this week, what would it be? Is this a difficult choice for you? Remember, you would not be able to watch any movies on television or download movies from websites. Why do you choose the movie you choose?

2. If you could see an episode of your favorite television show only once (because you cannot tape it or download it), what would that episode be? You must watch the episode in real-time when the show is on the network. (This cannot be a one-time sports event; it should be a normal scripted network show that appears on schedule every week). Why did you choose this show?

3. If you knew that your audience could access your television show or movie (or a filmed version of your book) only once, would you write your material differently? In what way?

4. Do you think your idea will appeal to audiences on all levels of transmedia platforms? Why? What is special about your material that will hold a viewer's attention?

5. Would your material be best suited for the large screen, television screen, computer or mobile screens? Why?

6. Do you think your material has the potential to appeal to all generations — even those that want to watch television in real-time?

EXERCISE

A MYSTERIOUS MILLIONAIRE

Identify the ways different generations consume popular culture. Take a well-known piece of content, such as F. Scott Fitzgerald's 1925 novel *The Great Gatsby*, and research the popularity of the book when it was first released and throughout subsequent decades. Then, identify the four feature film adaptations that have been produced since the book's publication and research how well those versions have been accepted by their contemporary audiences. Think about the future of this material — will Baz Luhrmann's 2013 version hold up against the other versions and through the ages? Could (or should) there be another version for the future?

CHAPTER 2

FRAGMEN- TATION

Due to our transmedia universe, we now have a fragmentation of audience — meaning, whether you are writing a novel, a web series, or poetry, it is a sure bet that you probably will not have 100% of the attention of your reader/viewer at all times. This fragmentation will only continue to expand in the future, so get used to it.

Audiences are consuming a variety of different content — entertainment based content along with news and sports content — and sometimes all at once. Understanding how audiences consume material assists the writer in knowing how to construct content.

WE'RE NOT GETTING THE WHOLE PICTURE ANY LONGER

So in addition to the pure fact that our attention is divided most of the time when we are consuming media, it is also the case that many of our texts within said media are also divided. They are convoluted and presented in a way that doesn't always make sense to all viewers, no matter when they are consuming the texts. Let me explain.

WAS IT AN EVOLUTION OF DANCE, OR RATHER A CONFUSION OF DANCE?

One of the first examples of both the origins and results of writing for a transmedia marketplace appeared in April of 2006. Mega "consumer-created content" provider YouTube was in its infancy. One of the first viral videos seen on YouTube is a video entitled "The Evolution of Dance" by Judson Laipply. Laipply, an "inspirational comedian," presented a video of himself dancing. He begins with Elvis Presley's 1956 "Hound Dog" as his start to this video that displays his obvious love of dancing to popular songs and the various different types of dances that have emerged over the years. The songs that follow are a menu of greatest hits from The Bee Gees to AC/DC to Michael Jackson, ranging from the mid-'50s to the mid-'00s.

The word "evolution" means advancement, growth, and progress, and my immediate thought was that he would present just that — an evolution of dance, meaning a display of one dance move over the other to show how dance moves had progressed through the years and through different types of music. He begins with two '60s hits, then moves to the '70s, and it soon became apparent to me that this was not an evolution of dance at all, but just a hodgepodge of songs and dances thrown together at random. He then includes hits from the '80s, '90s, and the '00s and while the video is entertaining, it is also misleading. And here's why.

As an individual who is aware of these pop hits, I am able to place the different genres of music in their proper decade, and because I lived through most of these decades, I know where each of these musicians appears within the history of music. However, any individuals who are viewing this video who were born in the '70s onward may or may not be aware of these songs and may watch this video and think that *Saturday Night*

Fever (1978) happened before *The Brady Bunch* (1970) and *Willy Wonka and the Chocolate Factory* (1971). Think about it; the viewer may take away an incorrect fact that those repetitive opening beats of, say, a song like "Ice Ice Baby" (1990), appeared at a different time in music history than it actually did.

REFERENCES ARE COMPLETELY OFF

We do not have any base upon which to work with if much of our media is just randomly put together without explanation. And in the world of accessing information and media via the web without any guidance or within any context, individuals are accessing information without direction or knowledge of what may have happened historically in that genre. I'm not criticizing Mr. Laipply for presenting an entertaining and popular video (at one time the most-watched clip on YouTube). However, if he really wanted to present a video showing the "evolution of dance," then he should have presented these songs and their dances in a chronological manner. That way we are entertained and we learn something at the same time — especially for those viewers who are young and impressionable and may not know the chronological history of our media.

MASHED UP

This is just a small example of what happens when content gets mashed up via the web. Because of our transmedia platforms, references to previous texts in pop culture are used all of the time and, in most cases, they are used out of context. And while this has always occurred within our media, at no time has it occurred at such a rapid speed and in so many different ways across all of our types of media. And at no time in the past have so many younger generations accessed media out of context than in this transmedia arena. The result is that there are generations of viewers/consumers who do not have a clue as to the origins of many of our pop culture content and texts.

I'm not condemning this, however. I am bringing to your attention how much more fragmented the audiences are today than they ever have been — and audiences are only going to continue to fall apart from each other. In many cases, writers who write for one specific group or generation are unaware of this disconnect between generations — and this works for older to younger writers and younger to older writers just the same — and because of this fact writers are sometimes unable to sell certain projects for a variety of reasons based on misunderstanding and confusion from their isolated point of view.

For instance, if you are a writer in your fifties and you are describing your main character in a medical drama for a television series and you say that he is similar to Hawkeye Pierce, you run the risk of losing your pitch because many folks in development who are in their twenties and thirties have no idea who Hawkeye Pierce — the famous lead character from the movie (1970) and television series (1972–83) *M.A.S.H.* — is. You would do better to refer to your main character as being similar to McDreamy from *Grey's Anatomy* (2005–present). Your potential buyers will understand that reference. And just the same, if you are in your twenties and pitching a reality series and you want to refer to previous shows that featured audiences being tricked via a camera and you only know *Punk'd* (2003–2007) and not the granddaddy of these types of shows, *Candid Camera* (1948–2004), then again, you may lose your pitch as there may be some individuals to whom you are pitching who may be aware of the history of that type of reality show.

And yes, even something as simple as one video featuring popular dances on YouTube can mess up an entire generation for the future. Now multiply this example times a million per hour and you can see how writing in a transmedia world can be a very confusing place to be. As a writer within this arena, you'll need to be aware of past texts that have addressed your subject matter. For now, no matter what your age or place in history might be, knowing the generational breakdowns will assist you overall in fine-tuning your material.

GENERATIONAL GAP

Sociologists have labeled current American generations as follows:

1900–1924 — G.I. Generation
1925–1945 — Silent Generation
1946–1964 — Baby Boomers
1965–1979 — Generation X
1980–2000 — Millennials or Generation Y
2000/2001–Present — New Silent Generation or Generation Z

Locate your generation. Identify at least one person that you know in other generations if you are able to. This will help you later on in your writing process when you are developing and researching your content, and also when you are constructing your pitch and selling materials.

SOME BRIEF NOTES ABOUT EACH GENERATION

I do not intend to make this a study in sociology, but I do want to point out some basic elements of each generation so you have an awareness of who you are writing for. Remember, all generations access all media, no matter what type of media you are constructing, whether it is a book, movie, TV series, or web series. Also, you may be writing a movie script, but eventually that movie will be accessible via television and the web in different large and small and mobile screen versions and by different sets of consumers. Know that the way one group of viewers consumes your work may or may not translate to another group of viewers. Being aware of this entire picture helps you in being a better writer.

1925–1945 — Silent Generation
1900–1924 — G.I. Generation

This generation reflects those individuals who do remember when media was unfragmented. They remember where they were when the first radio shows were heard and when television was born. They watched television in real-time, went to movies when their local movie theaters changed their weekly selection, and read newspapers daily. Today they still consume television (both broadcast and cable) in real-time for the most part, are the least likely generation to pay to see movies in theaters, and hang on to reading the few newspapers that still exist and enjoy reading novels/books in general. This is a generation that is set in their ways. If any of them have adapted to the digital age, they do so because they wish to keep in touch with their grandchildren.

1946–1964 — Baby Boomers

Hovering a bit beyond and around the mid-century mark, this generation has lived half of their lives without the convenience of computers and two decades (give or take a couple years) with the advantage of the digital age. For the most part, they have adapted to fragmented media. They were raised on the Golden Age of Television ('50s–'70s), enjoyed the dawn of cable broadcasting, and can remember iconic videos on MTV. Boomers have embraced the use of computers and mobile devices. They still go to movies in theaters, however they have been known to enjoy marathon viewings of popular television shows. They read print books or digital versions on their tablets and utilize SMS texts to communicate, although emailing is a major way for them to keep in touch.

1965–1979 — Generation X

Many of this generation have more in common with the Baby Boomers because they were raised without computers. If we use the date of 1993 as the last full year of print-only communication and look to around that same time as the time when home computers first appeared in many households, the math results are that these folks were in their late teens to twenties before accessing media via digital ways and means. Therefore, they have a vague idea of what it might have been like before a transmedia world existed. They certainly understand cable and blockbuster movie releases and have adapted wholeheartedly to the digital age, as their children are now being raised with computers. This is the generation that also understands what goes into "consumer-created content" because they have been creating their own content along with consuming commercial content since their twenties.

1980–2000 — Millennials or Generation Y
2000/2001–Present — New Silent Generation or Generation Z

These generations have, for the most part, grown up completely with computers and the digital age. They know how to instantly access the web for information and they know how to create content. They process media at lightning speeds and access every mobile device they have on hand. Information and all content is available at all times via their cellphones and tablets via apps and other mobile platforms. They are not on a path to find their answers. There is no path, for they have already arrived. They've arrived and are eager to both create and consume media and content 24/7. They are changing the way media is consumed, completely embracing binge watching via Netflix and downloading movies whenever they wish.

They go to movies for the experience of the event flick, texting throughout the movie so they can share their thoughts within their social media forums. Their entire life has been available via social media platforms such as Facebook and they have shared all of their favorite media with all of their social networks via the web.

As we can see, even in these brief summaries of media behavior per each generation, Baby Boomers consume media differently than Millennials, etc. There are always exceptions within these groups. There is an excellent website to access to know more about the generations who have been born past that 1993 date. It is Ypulse at *ypulse.com*. If you are from one of the generations pre-Millennials and Gen Y, this site is essential for you to understand how media is consumed. For those of you from the Gen Y and Millennial group, the site is also important, as it reports on both traditional and transmedia platforms.

SO THERE YOU HAVE IT

It is my hope that now you can see why those of the Gen X and younger generations viewing "The Evolution of Dance" video may be misguided regarding its content. Additionally, by being aware of the way media has been radically altered by technology and how it is consumed, we begin to see how certain generations may not understand references to popular culture due to where they exist in that said culture. We'll continue to examine this in upcoming chapters. For now, do you plan to binge watch *Orange Is The New Black* on Netflix this evening, or watch an episode of *Duck Dynasty* in real-time? Depending on your answer, I bet I could guess what generation you're a part of.

TOOLKIT SANDBOX

A Sailor Man, Some Questions, and Some Old People In Love

CASE STUDY: POPEYE THE SAILOR MAN

Popeye The Sailor Man, a comic that first appeared in newspapers in 1929, enjoyed popularity throughout most of the 20th century. It went from a newspaper comic to a theatrical cartoon series in 1933. The character was also featured within a radio series between 1935–38. Popeye's likeability continued to grow and, in 1938, the adventures of this sailor who is capable of coming up with untangled solutions to problems he and his friends encounter, earned him the label of being Hollywood's most popular cartoon character at the time. The last of the 125 theatrical shorts was produced in 1957 and went into television syndication. A syndicated cartoon series was developed in 1960 and 200 episodes aired over two years. In 1978 *The All New Popeye Hour* debuted as part of CBS's Saturday morning children's programming lineup and ran until 1983.

In 1980 a film musical entitled *Popeye*, starring Robin Williams as the title character, met with mixed reviews. In 2004, for the 75th anniversary of the cartoon, *Popeye's Voyage: A Search for Pappy*, a computer-animated feature, was released on DVD. To this day, Popeye is being broadcast and consumed. The franchise will enter the public domain in 2025.

Through this short run on the history of this franchise, you can see how those creators and consumers who enjoyed the comic strip in the '30s–'50s went on to create newer versions for the '80s. However, since the early '80s Popeye and his pals haven't exactly been seen at the top of box office or television or even comic strip lists. Here, unlike *The Wonderful Wizard of Oz*, we see a franchise that, while still active, has not played much of a role in popular culture in the last thirty-plus years.

In 2010 Sony Pictures Animation announced that they would produce a new version of Popeye. Their plans are to present the content as a CGI, 3D adaptation with Genndy Tartakovsky (he has a background in cable series animation and directed the 2012 animated favorite *Hotel Transylvania*). The question is, can a talented director and featured animated special effects save this franchise that has been for the most part out of the public consciousness for so long? In other words, will the techniques so often utilized in action films such as 3D save a storyline that simply may not be relatable to 21st century audiences?

The film, currently slated for 2015, has already suffered a number of setbacks over the past few years. Due to its lack of popularity over the last two decades, this is an example of how execs need to carefully evaluate concepts within popular culture. How adaptable is the storyline to contemporary consumers? Is there anything within the storyline that can relate to young consumers? If the creators are relying on visual effects and techniques, that's not enough. There's another animated character that is in a similar situation — Mr. Magoo. Made hugely popular through a series of theatrical short cartoons and television series throughout the 1950s and '60s, Mr. Magoo has had very little exposure during the past few decades. Since an unsuccessful 1997 movie version starring Leslie Nielsen as Magoo, this once-iconic character has barely registered on the pop culture charts.

If a franchise is not kept up to date, there is very little that can resurrect it, unless you the writer can find a way to make it relevant within today's current (and future) marketplace.

QUESTIONING WITH THE WRITER'S ADVANTAGE

1. Do you see your idea appealing to audiences beyond just your peer group?

2. How would your grandparents view your work? Would they understand it?

3. How would your younger siblings (or children) view your work? Would they care about what you are saying?

4. Do you understand how different ages/generations might find your work to be interesting?

5. Do you understand how different ages/generations might find your work to be dull — or how they simply might not understand it?

6. Have you ever found yourself questioning the chronological order of a specific genre, wanting to know how the genre evolved and being fascinated by artists within the genre that inspired one another?

7. Do you think you can create a piece of content that will appeal to all generations?

EXERCISE

THE NOTEBOOK

Nicholas Sparks' novel *The Notebook* (1996) has been highly popular among Gen X and Millennial readers, yet the story involves an aged couple dealing with health issues. Research why and how this seemingly Baby Boomer-orientated book and movie appeals to younger generations.

CHAPTER 3

TRANSMEDIA

As digital technology continues to refine itself, media in the 21st century is undergoing many changes. On one hand, stagnation exists with so many sequels, prequels, spin-offs, reboots, and remakes of already tested content, while on the other hand there are so many new opportunities for writers. Lets look at how we have arrived at this point in the transmedia marketplace. From that perch there will emerge a cornucopia of new and unique writing opportunities not to be missed by writers following The Writer's Advantage.

PUBLISHING IN A TRANSMEDIA WORLD

The publishing world remains steady in that new writers will always have the same opportunities to write within the tried and true genres that have existed for years. For instance: Romance, Mystery, Women's Fiction, Self-Help books are mainstays. The Young Adult market, however, has presented itself as an emerging arena — so much so that a new genre entitled "New Adult" has been established.

New Adult is a term that is used when 1.) a Young Adult book begins to attract older (18–25) young adults, and/or 2.) a book designed for the Young Adult market crosses over into the mainstream — a book such as *The Hunger Games* (2008), for instance. Actually, it was the extreme success of books like *The Hunger Games* trilogy that lead to the publishing industry realizing that authors appealing to the Gen X and Millennial markets could break out beyond just those readers. New Adult protagonists deal with the same issues that Young Adult protagonists deal with, however with a bit more of a realization of what life is all about from a wizened post-teenage perspective. The publishing world needed to identify and brand for this new group of readers. The fiction world is now divided between older (25–65+) readers and younger (18–25) readers. Many of these titles have addressed topics with sexual identity and LGBT issues, drinking and drug use and its legalization, economic and job-finding scenarios, immigrant rights — in other words, issues that many within the 18–25 age range currently deal with on a daily basis. These issues are not always shared with the older reading population who may have more difficulty relating to these scenarios. This existence of a new genre proves that writers can make changes in media. And, should a Young Adult title break out into the mainstream reading population, it would probably do so because there is something within the book that resonates to all ages on the universal human need scale. This is something to think about when you are composing your new novel. The publishing industry will embrace a new genre when it attracts large reading populations — and you could be the writer to establish that new genre. The onslaught of self-publishing and digital publishing has also led to changes in the industry. Digital books are surpassing the sales of paperbacks in some genres. Mystery, Romance, Sci-Fi and Young Adult are all genres that do well in a downloaded world — mostly due to their dedicated fans. See if you can create your whole new genre for a specific group of readers.

MOVIE TRANSITION IN A TRANSMEDIA WORLD

Movie industry pre-awareness of titles and characters has dominated the marketplace, resulting in a glut of sequels, prequels, remakes, and reboots. This is a commercial world where very few authentic ideas exist. Movies now feature "trailer moments" — most often things being destroyed. When budgets for movies reach well above $100 million, it seems that the storyline has to include blowing up something to save the world. Blockbusters have played themselves out. So the question now stands: Where do we go from here?

There are a number of reasons for this phenomenon. One of the biggest reasons is that we now have a preponderance of fanboys writing these types of movies. Not all screenwriters possess basic writing skill sets. Instead of knowing how to construct characters with depth, complex storylines and meaningful dialogue, they really only know how to construct one-dimensional characters and plots based solely on what is known within a thin pop culture realm. They are writing from a fragmented viewpoint — as they have rarely taken the time to study the history of, say, a superhero or well-known genre, and are writing based on what they and their peers know — which is only what has been known from trailers and commercials, sequels and forums, and spin-offs and reboots that display and discuss the material.

We have had twenty years of writers raised on content that has been based on previous content. It is no wonder why there are very few new, authentic ideas. The death of the original screenplay happened a while ago. Additionally, many of these action-heavy films are dominated by directors — not writers — and their vision for the screen. The result, sometimes known as "Chaos Cinema," is a great amount of digital destruction versus story. Unintelligible sensory overload abides in this arena and the result is a sad state of modern action, and what was once known as the big blockbuster film comes and goes in our theaters without much fanfare — or box office success. We have lost the construction of an authentic storyline, and without story, movies can't exist. We need to make movies that are well researched, feature characters with depth, complex storylines, and yes, meaningful dialogue based on the building blocks of their genre.

TV AND THE TRANSMEDIA WORLD

The days of real-time television watching are gone. The days of appointment television — where one would make a note of the day and time of a specific show to be watched — are gone also.

Broadcast networks especially are losing adult viewers under fifty. Why? Because in a transmedia marketplace the viewer can consume television content anytime they want via any mode they wish. The result is that network shows aren't what they used to be. How does a network appeal to the vast public, the public once known as mass media viewers, when those viewers no longer exist?

This is why we've seen the decline of long-form television content such as miniseries and "Movies of the Week," and in fact the only types of television content that can appeal to all demographics are religious-themed, fantasy, or music-based. We've seen the great success of cable networks and the chances they have taken with iconic series such as *The Sopranos* (1999–2007), *Mad Men* (2007–present), *Breaking Bad*

(2008–2013), and *Game of Thrones* (2011–present), to name just a few, and that trend will continue... and it will continue on the television screen, computer screen, tablet screen, and smartphone screen.

TELEVISION'S THIRD GOLDEN AGE

The trend in television is the opposite of what we are seeing within the movie industry. Writers are embracing complex characters and sordid storylines. That's all good. In fact, after the first wave of television programming in the 1950s, considered TVs Golden Age, and then again in the 1980s, when we saw the dawn of the serialized procedural dramas and new classic comedies, the writing for television has just been getting better and better. Perhaps this is because television writers must concentrate on their well-formed complex characters in order to have the storylines move forward on a week-by-week, or episode-by-episode, level. The difference is so plain and clear — less gets blown up within a television series, and the writer tends to concentrate on the development of the characters from which storylines emerge.

So it is proven that audiences want nutritious programming — they'll watch it via the networks and websites, heck, they'll even binge watch it when they get addicted to it. And they'll watch it again and again. There are fans of *Downton Abbey* (2010–present) who watch the entire series over again every season as they anticipate the new season. This is the way content should be consumed — with a fanatical enthusiasm. The creators of these series are to be applauded. They are generating content that displays their expertise of their genre. The television industry is light years ahead of the film side.

That said, networks and advertisers need to broaden their focus beyond the 18-to-49 marketplace. We now have a connected world of DVDs, DVRs, Video-On-Demand, and web streaming. And guess what? The combination of all of these various ways of media are more powerful than the mass media template ever was.

TALK OF THE TOWN

In the days before consumers could manipulate the way they would consume content, a popular show would run in real-time and the following day everyone would talk about it around the water cooler, or Xerox machine, at work. This action became known as "water cooler conversation." When the audience is fragmented, as we know it now is, it is difficult to discuss a piece of content the next day after viewing the show because everyone is viewing the show at different times in different ways. "Spoiler alerts" have to be announced in most cases in case someone in the crowd hasn't watched said content. As a result, the water cooler scenario has moved online, and mostly to Twitter.

Twitter buzz — chatter posted while a show is being broadcast (usually on cable), has been known to boost TV show ratings. This works for the remaining shows that appear on regular broadcast and cable television schedules *and* when series appear on Netflix for the first days or week. As more and more con-sumers gorge themselves with marathon viewings of series on Netflix and Amazon, binge watching becomes more and more popular. Add to this the Twitter dialogue of one or two popular celebrities or digital mavens and the series' cache is elevated to high levels. In some cases, those folks who "cut the cord" from traditional cable companies are returning to cable because they want to be part of the "it's happening now" experience.

There has been a large amount of viewers who chose to go rogue and view television content via their own time, place, and venue. The model for television content is evolving. One wonders why broadcast networks are obsessed with the traditional TV pilot system. The question should be "Why even have a new fall season at all?" within this transmedia arena. (Since the dawn of television, broadcast networks have operated on a system that includes a period of time called "Pilot Season," usually held in January through April of a new year. This is when development departments choose and develop pilots — as in the series' first show that will "take off" into a new series, chosen from pitches they would have been listening to since mid-year the previous year. Network execs then choose which of the pilots they want to go to series and those series appear to much fanfare and publicity in the fall of every year, when viewership picks up again after summer breaks, hence the "New Fall Season." This process has never been followed by cable networks — they pretty much use the process of "throw it up against the wall and if it sticks, we'll make more episodes" — in other words, they do not have money to develop ideas and produce pilots, they just shoot on a low budget and run it on their networks. If consumers like it, they make more. As the transmedia universe continues to grow, this remains the template used to move forward with new material to be shown on traditional TV.)

TV creativity continues to be boosted through new models and setups. There is and will continue to be internet-delivered television — not internet television (meaning television networks as we know it accessed on the web), but the internet will be your sole source of television content. This opens up a wide field of content creation for writers. You no longer have to think in any of the traditional models of seasons or pilot episodes. Think about it. There are so many opportunities for you to explore where you might want to go with your characters and storylines.

TRANSMEDIA SUMMARY

In closing, no matter if you are writing the next new genre novel, a screenplay, or TV series, you still need to do your homework. As future writers embrace their genres, they will master the future of that genre and not fall into the age-old scenario of re-writing what has already been done and providing mash-up nonsensical versions of classic texts. Let's create some original pieces of content for this new digital landscape.

TOOLKIT SANDBOX

A Woman in Pigtails, Some Questions, and Could There Ever Be Another Wonderful Life?

CASE STUDY: COME BACK, *MARY HARTMAN, MARY HARTMAN*

Mary Hartman, Mary Hartman (1976–78) was a syndicated soap opera parody well ahead of its time, created and produced by Norman Lear. The main character, Mary Hartman, played by Louise Lasser, took the viewer into her world — and what a world it was. As in any good parody, the storylines played off of the usual soap opera palette — infidelity, mistrust, characters who didn't know who their real fathers were, and the waxy yellow build-up on her kitchen floor. This show appeared five days a week in first-run syndication, usually after the local nightly news on affiliates across America. That alone made the show different, the fact that it was a parody of a type of show that would usually air in the late mornings/early afternoons made this a unique piece of television programming late at night. It was a bit of a programming experiment, but Lear had a good reputation at that time after producing mega primetime hits such as *All in the Family* (1971–1979), *Maude* (1972–1978), *The Jeffersons* (1975–1985), *One Day at a Time*

(1975–1984), and *Good Times* (1974–1979), to name a few. Many of the story arcs included exploring the woman's role in the household — whether or not she should initiate sex or have a career, and other feminist topics of the times. Shot with three cameras, soap opera style, and on limited sets, the show deliberately mimicked the soap opera genre. The actors perfected "the pause" — a dramatically extended moment where a plot question is left unanswered until after the commercial break. The storylines became near-to-ridiculous, but that was why you watched the show. It was a hyper-version of a well-known genre, and it hit a nerve among viewers at the time. The show offered refreshment among a stale offering of late-night entertainment and has gone unchallenged, except perhaps for the brilliant *Arrested Development* (2003–present) as far as parody and tongue-in-cheek entertainment goes.

The show ended in 1978. To this day it has one of the largest cult followings of any TV show. Could it have survived the '80s and '90s and eventually the 21st century? Probably not, as it would not have been able to sustain the level of comedic intelligence it put forth five days a week. It was an exquisite serving of clever television that was later followed by its sequel, *Fernwood Tonight*, which only lasted a few months in the summer of 1977 and featured characters from *Mary Hartman, Mary Hartman*. My bet is that a series like this could find an audience today via a web series. There would be enough viewers who would understand the soap opera parody aspect and who could also appreciate the level of mock admiration that went into a show like this. Watch it for yourself. In fact, use this example as a way to watch other texts with the question of "Would this idea work today?"

QUESTIONING WITH THE WRITER'S ADVANTAGE

1. Is there a type of book, movie, or TV show that you think may need to be labeled as a new genre or sub-genre within its genre? If so, identify and name it.

2. Name the last blockbuster film that you found to be less than entertaining. Why?

3. Could you re-imagine that blockbuster film by adding a stronger storyline? Three-dimensional characters? Strong dialogue? In other words, could that film have been saved? How?

4. What was the last series you binge watched? What made you want to continue to watch the next episode after the last one, and the next one and the next one?

5. What kind of entertainment programming would broadcast networks have to provide in order for you to watch that programming in real-time?

6. What advice do you have for studios for them to make better movies?

7. What advice do you have for networks for them to make better television shows?

EXERCISE

COULD THERE EVER BE ANOTHER
WONDERFUL LIFE?

Re-image the 1946 Capra film *It's A Wonderful Life* for today's marketplace. (You can work with the material as a prequel, sequel, remake, or reboot.)

CHAPTER 4

WITH SO MANY OPTIONS, WHAT'S A 21ST CENTURY WRITER TO DO?

So you think your idea for a new vampire novel is a good one? Think again.

Nine times out of ten your idea is really quite mediocre and it has been done before, actually a number of times and in a number of different ways. And get this, there's also a possibility that an even better version of your idea already exists.

Sorry to have to burst your bubble, but agents, managers, publishers, folks who work at production companies, and any type of potential buyer does not want to be bothered with material that's just ordinary. They have seen it all. They have read manuscripts that didn't get made — often for good reasons — and they have heard pitches, read loglines and synopses and treatments for thousands of ideas. They have attended screenings of films that haven't found distribution and have heard pitches at dozens of pitch fests and have taken pitch meetings daily throughout the years. These folks are not practicing their game — they are playing hardball. They want to win in this competitive market and they are looking for material they can win with.

They are not interested in anyone who is writing as a hobby. They want to work with talented, informed writer/creators who know where their material is going to fit in the marketplace. They want to broker a deal with you to make money for themselves, their company, and you. This is the real thing. Do not waste their time pitching a mediocre idea — pitch them an authentic idea that will complement and perhaps even change the course of your genre, and in turn, their company and overall reputation.

So, if you are going to sell your work in today's competitive marketplace, and if you want to stand out within that marketplace, you need to utilize the Genre Toolkit List as illustrated within the next few chapters and follow it as you write or re-write your material, or re-think your pitch for your authentic text. You need your game plan to be in place. You need to think like they think. You need to know what they know.

THREE QUESTIONS

Development execs and editors all ask the same three basic questions when evaluating material to be published or produced and those questions are:

Why make this?

Why make this now?

Who cares?

Often the difference between an ordinary idea and a selling idea are found in the answers to the above questions. In other words, you'll need to be prepared to answer these questions — and answer them efficiently. By doing the research and following the steps within the next chapters, you'll discover the answers to these three important questions for your genre, your material, and your pitch.

At the very base of every idea, the idea will be evaluated for its own merit. Why make this movie? Why publish this book? Why make this TV series? Yes, the basic answer is "because readers/viewers will like it," sure, but that's not enough. What is it about the idea that makes it unique, compelling, and authentic compared to all other competing ideas in your genre... and then, placed within the time frame of when the idea is being evaluated: Why make this movie *now*? Why publish this book *now*? Why make this TV series *now*?

THE NOW FACTOR

You will find that knowing the history of your genre and current trends will assist you in answering the "now" questions. In other words, if you have an idea for a western and you would have been preparing to pitch that idea after the release of the Jerry Bruckheimer/Johnny Depp *The Lone Ranger* fiasco (Summer, 2013), then clearly the "now" factor comes into play. Because that movie experienced colossal financial loss for its studio and bombed with both critics and audiences, it will be quite some time before studios begin looking at westerns seriously again. It does not matter how good your script is, you'll need to give it a little rest and let it sit on a shelf for a while. It is often that the "now" element can kill an idea as the marketplace is just not right for that idea at the time you pitch it.

WHO CARES, WHO REALLY CARES?

Finally, the question "Who cares?" Yes, it sounds crass, it sounds like I'm asking you to just disregard your idea, but I am seriously asking you to ask this question about your idea. Who really will care about your material? Remember, they need to care enough to want to purchase it — whether it be a book, a download, a box office ticket, or the time watching on TV or downloading through the internet. This is not just about the group of fans or a group with a particular affiliation, this is about who will *pay* to consume your material.

Think about this.

Think about this closely.

A "BABY AT 43" PITCH

Let me give you an example of a pitch and how the "now" and "Who cares?" elements fall into place. As someone who has developed a great deal of programming for women's audiences, I have heard an eternity of pitches featuring women as victims, survivors, single mothers, etc. If someone pitches me a story about a 43-year-old unmarried woman who has had a successful career in advertising or law or pharmaceuticals (whatever field), and decides at the last minute of her biological clock's ticking that she wants to have a child... I will wait for the writer to tell me the rest of the story.

And there is no rest of the story, because in their mind, that is their story.

To which I say "Who cares?" Seriously, who will care about that storyline? No one. We have seen numerous movies about women wanting to have children later in life. I could produce a list at least two pages long consisting of movies with this plotline. Why make that movie (now)? It has been made and no one will care (now).

However, if the writer pitches me an idea and starts out in the same way — one of the main characters is a 43-year-old single business woman having her first child and at the same time, her 22-year-old niece is also having her first child — because the niece does not see the benefit of having a career and only wants to be supported by a rich husband — I suddenly see some conflict here. I see that there could arise an interesting plot as the two women proceed through the experience of having a child and discover many realizations about themselves, each other, and life in general. As the older woman warns the younger woman that she'll need skills if the man ever leaves her, the younger woman reminds the older woman how lonely her life has been in the boardroom, and so on and so forth. Now I can provide an answer to why make this movie now — because there are many women experiencing these scenarios in today's contemporary society.

I can also provide an answer to the "Who cares?" question and that is that a good number of viewers will care — both those in the Gen X and Baby Boomer segments and Millennials alike. This is an idea that spans generations and therefore captures a larger viewership. The idea now works on a number of levels and provides a topic that reflects basic human needs and wants. This is an example of an authentic idea.

AUTHENTIC IDEAS

It is all too often that a writer pitches an exact idea that has been done before. All ideas have been executed before in some form or manner, but not all writers are aware of how the idea has been executed and that fact often leads to an element of naivety on behalf of the writer. The fact that all ideas have been seen previous to your being aware of them is actually a good thing. Why? Because you have something to base your work on, something to compare your work to. You can do your research and see how an idea such as yours has been executed by other creatives who have tackled the subject matter previously. You'll learn how gathering this info helps with your own processing of your idea and ultimate end product. I've seen way too many writers develop, write, and pitch ideas that they shouldn't have even started. Their idea was doomed from the very beginning, and mostly because they decided to write with blinders on. They didn't seek out the history of their genre or embrace the marketplace they intend to enter.

WHAT WE NEED

Agents, editors, and development people all work within their specific arenas, with their specific genres, and will some- times list what they are looking for in general. I repeat — IN GENERAL. Don't ask them "What are you looking for?" That question aggravates them. And besides, you already know the answer. The answer is that they are looking for the next huge mega best-selling book, blockbuster movie, or acclaimed tele- vision series that will have viewers binge watching over and over. They want the next big thing, the next mega piece of pop culture, the next franchise. So instead of asking, now you know, and so let's keep moving forward so that you can intelligently create that next piece of pop culture that every development person wants to purchase.

WONDERMENT

What we need is a sense of "wonderment." Wonderment is that indescribable essence of your favorite book or movie or TV show. Wonderment is necessary in all forms of writing. It is what speaks to you alone as you read the book or view the filmed visuals. It is that energy that connects our collective consciousness. It is what takes you out of your own world and transports you to the world you are experiencing. It is what you get out of having read the book, viewed the movie or TV show. Wonderment is a wonderful thing. Most texts that stand the test of time or resonate to groups of consumers have this ele- ment of wonderment, and that is what makes them different.

Think about adding wonderment to your material — what is it that the audience will get from experiencing your idea that they ordinarily would not have the opportunity to experience?

Answer this and you are halfway toward moving your idea from mediocre to magnificent.

WHAT WE DON'T NEED

We do not need any more sequels, prequels, remakes, reboots, CGI, VFX, or green screen activity, and we need to stop composing storylines that are so weak and one-dimensional that they can be told entirely in a movie trailer.

We also do not need to be creating, writing, and pitching ideas that have been done before in the same way that they have previously appeared— or worse, create, write, and pitch ideas without knowing the history of the genre.

NAIVE OR JUST PLAIN STUPID?

Often there's a naive enthusiasm that writers display when presenting their work. They are so excited about their material that they often forget to stop and explore what is behind their work. I know this seems almost impossible to understand. You're saying "But I've worked on writing this manuscript/script for months and/or years, of course I know what my storyline and genre is about." But in most cases writers do not know. The result is an ineffective pitch and a lack of their own authentic voice.

"STORMY WEATHER" PITCHES

One of the best ways to explain this is to share the wisdom of an *American Idol* (2002–present) mentor. During the 2013 season, Harry Connick Jr. was brought in to mentor the aspiring singers partaking in the singing competition for that round. A talented young woman, Kree Harrison, sang the classic song "Stormy Weather." Kree presented an interpretation of the song that may now be referred to as the "Idol fixation"

— when artists use vocal tricks and fancy techniques to sing the song instead of truly understanding the meaning of the lyrics. Harry's reaction and feedback consisted of his asking her if she knew what she was singing about. He went on to explain that the lyrics express a woman's feelings as she is in the throes of depression, she's missing her lover, she's definitely feeling the blues. Harry asked Kree what kind of singer she wants to be and told her that if she wants to be a great singer, she'll need to sing the song and utilize the melody the way it was intended. Finally, he suggested that she go back and listen to classic versions of the song — timeless interpretations that never failed to connect with listeners.

Kree sang well, but her interpretation of the song's text did not captivate and connect. Harry's mentoring advice was excellent. Sure, this is just an interpretation of a song, however, it is an excellent example of moving forward with your creativity without knowing anything about what has gone on before within your genre. Don't do this. Don't look like an idiot when delivering your interpretation of a genre. Know what has happened previously, otherwise your material, your presentation, and your pitch will be a "Stormy Weather Pitch," and those in the know, will know.

TOOLKIT SANDBOX

Oh!, To Be Like Your Idol, Some Questions, and Rebooting The Remake?

CASE STUDY: LYNCHIAN, SPIELBERG-LIKE, AND TARANTINO-ESQUE

The term "lynchian" has come to be known as having the same balance between the macabre and the mundane, a path that is often found in the works of filmmaker David Lynch. David

Lynch's body of work, from *Eraserhead* (1977) to *Blue Velvet* (1986) to *Mulholland Drive* (2001) (among many others) illustrates the filmmaker's view of the world that most would say is surrealistic. However, it is very much grounded in the everyday scenarios that we all live in. Within the opening moments of *Blue Velvet*, small town, Main Street U.S.A. is alive in all of its rich Technicolor glory, until the camera pans to the grass, and then lower within the grass to find a severed bloody ear. This is to say that not everything is as perfect as it seems and if we look below the surface, we'll find some horrific truths. Lynch likes to play with that fine line between mundane and macabre, knowing that the macabre wins out many more times than none. Lynch states that foreign film directors were his greatest influences, such as Stanley Kubrick, Werner Herzog, and Jacques Tati. It is a well known fact that 20th century foreign film directors were known for their gritty scenes of reality and that war-torn European scenarios and backdrops were more in-your-face than in the work of most American film directors. Lynch's subject matter, scene set-ups, use of black & white and color along with murky realness are clearly just extensions of these master filmmakers' brilliant visions.

Spielberg's influences include Brits Alfred Hitchcock and David Lean, but they also include very American directors such as John Ford, Frank Capra, and Howard Hawks. Spielberg's stories reflect American values, even when the subject matter isn't strictly "American." They are linear in execution, have morals, and illustrate what is right and wrong. His movies explore questions that Americans have faced throughout history and he attempts to answer those questions through his masterful storytelling, cinematic direction, and solid character development. Spielberg has proven to be a follower in the great American directors' footsteps, carrying the torch of American filmmaking onward into the 21st century. The difference between Lynch's movies and Spielberg's movies are obvious, yet they were born in the same year and were exposed to the same media and popular culture during their formative years. Spielberg was born and raised in Cincinnati, Ohio, and spent time in New Jersey and Arizona. Lynch was born in Missoula, Montana, and his family traveled around a great deal. Their lives make up their art and this is clearly seen through their movies. Lynch takes his European influences and weaves them into his work while Spielberg stays closer to home within his work.

Now, as far as Quentin Tarantino's influences are concerned, his love of cinema begins at a very early age and includes many different types of genres and directors, from American *film noir* and "Grindhouse" to Asian action films. To get a full idea of the multitude of influences at work on Tarantino, visit What Culture!'s "Quentin Tarantino's Definitive Guide To Homages, Influences and References" at *whatculture.com*.

The main idea of this case study is to become aware of how artists influence artists and how those artists then carve and craft their own unique mark on their work. Do you see your work becoming influential to the point that there will be an "-ian" or "-like" or "-esque" after your name having an effect on future generations?

QUESTIONING WITH THE WRITER'S ADVANTAGE

1. Why make (publish, produce) your idea?
2. Why make (publish, produce) your idea now? (Focus on trends, audiences, fragmentation of audiences, etc., within your answers.)
3. Who is going to care about your idea? (Your answer will assist you with audience target marketing.)
4. Identify a moment or thread of wonderment in one of your favorite texts.

5. Do you have wonderment in your idea? (In other words, is the consumer going to get something from experiencing your work that they cannot get otherwise?)

6. Do you see your work becoming influential to the point that there will be an "-ian" or "-like" or "-esque" after your name having an effect on future generations?

7. What would Harry Connick Jr. (or any mentor in your field) say to you about your proposed idea? (WWHCJD?)

EXERCISE

REBOOT A REMAKE

Take a recent remake or reboot of a movie and compare and contrast the different versions of the material. How does each version relate to its audience and how does each version hold up as we move further into the 21st century? (Hint: Extra credit for examining major remake train wrecks such as Gus Van Sant's 1998 *Psycho* vs. Hitchcock's 1960 masterpiece.)

SECTION 2

ARMING YOURSELF

CHAPTER 5

THE GENRE TOOLKIT LIST

It's now time to get to know and utilize the elements of *The Writer's Advantage* Genre Toolkit. The elements of the Genre Toolkit List are discussed in detail in the next few chapters.

The Genre Toolkit List's 10 Steps are:

1. Identify your genre's quintessential text.
2. Identify the traits of your genre.
3. Identify the mass production history of your genre.
4. Analyze audience reaction of your genre — mass or cult?
5. Trends and patterns of your genre.
6. Make your checklist of traits you'll use.
7. What would an authentic text look like using all of your research? (The answer is your work.)
8. Defend your work.
9. What mastering your genre can do for you.
10. Learning how to answer the question "What else have you got?"

Utilizing and mastering this path assists you in getting your work out into the world.

This is the fun part. This is the time where you get to return to the days of your youth to recapture how it felt when you watched your first *Twilight Zone* (1959–1964) episode or read your first *Superman* comic (1938–present), or when you saw *Star Wars* (1977) or read *Harry Potter and the Sorcerer's Stone* (2001) for the first time. Writing should be an exhilarating experience, and the passion you had for a specific type of book or television series or comic, etc., is often one of the building blocks upon which you form your own writing style. Being aware of these roots will help you be a better writer and in constructing an authentic text.

So call upon all of those childhood and adolescent influences. Consciously or unconsciously they influence you and your writing for the rest of your life. (Hopefully some of the Toolkit Sandbox exercises have been helping you tap into this energy also.)

WHAT'S YOUR GENRE?

I'd like to explain why you need to locate and select your genre type — at least for your first few projects. Essentially, it's because the rest of the entertainment industry — publishing, visual, and digital alike — needs to know your genre in order to position and promote your work. The marketplace — both the buyers who will be evaluating your work, and the eventual consumers — will look to a certain genre and familiarities that they recognize. They will compare those elements with other projects and align them with others' work in your chosen genre. If you don't appear on the scene in a specific genre, the promotion-making machinery, along with the general public, will not know how to frame your work. They won't know what to do with it.

You'll have assistance from other writers and projects within your genre when you position yourself with those who have gone before you. Just visualize your novel, film, or web series under the "Also Suggested" list via Amazon or Netflix. And while you may have an aversion to having to use labels for your work, it is highly recommended that you go this route rather than to shrink behind the spotlight never to be heard from again if you insist that your work cannot be categorized. Identify your genre before going out to shop your idea.

Here is a list of main genres. They can be used in combination with one another as hybrids also.

GENRES

- Action-adventure
- Animation
- Anthology
- Biography
- Buddy Picture
- Comedy
- Coming of Age
- Crime Drama
- Docudrama
- Documentary
- Erotic Drama
- Family
- Fantasy
- Horror
- Historical
- Love Story/Romance
- Martial Arts
- Musical
- Mystery
- Political Drama
- Psychodrama
- Religious Drama
- Road Picture
- Romantic Comedy
- Satire
- Science Fiction
- Slasher
- Soap Opera
- Sports
- Sword & Sorcery
- Supernatural
- Suspense Thriller
- True Story
- War
- Western
- Youth

MORE ABOUT DEVELOPMENT DEPARTMENTS

In the previous chapter I mentioned the three questions potential buyers ask. Actually, the people who evaluate your work when you submit to an agency, producer, publisher, production company, web site, or financier — just about anyone who may be a potential buyer of the material — work within development departments of those companies. After you submit your work, someone is going to be evaluating your material beyond those three questions. They will be producing a document known as coverage. Coverage is a report, usually three to five pages in length. It is written as a record that that particular agency or production company, etc., has viewed and evaluated your work, and as a document that can be read by everyone in the company. In other words, the folks who are higher up on the food chain do not read every piece of material that is submitted. Readers (full-time and freelance), Script and Manuscript Analysts, Editors, and sometimes Interns are the folks who do the reading — the sifting and winnowing of all submitted material.

One of the first items they identify within your work is your genre. From there they evaluate your work as a piece within that genre. In other words, if you are writing a romantic comedy, they are familiar with the elements that make up a romantic comedy and are looking for those traits (we'll spend time with traits in Chapter 7), not the traits that are inherent to a western or comedy, etc. They will also often refer to other properties — mostly produced and well-known properties — that are within your genre to compare and contrast your work as a potential buy. If you do not know your genre, or you have written a piece that is not entirely sure what genre it falls into, then these analysts are going to have difficulty in identifying and discussing your work.

The analysts will continue to evaluate story elements such as character arcs, dialogue, structure, tone, writing quality, and some setting and production values, however they are mostly looking for commercial material. The bottom line is that they need to find lucrative product for their publishing company or network, etc., so they will be comparing and contrasting your work with the material previously and currently being produced within your genre. It is important that your good writing is on display. If a manuscript or script shows great potential to be commercially popular, you have an advantage. If your writing is strong and your idea is different, that too will attract positive accolades and that coverage will be circulated through the company and on to editors and producers and beyond. It is often at this stage in the process of submitting your work that potential buyers can already see why your material is authentic. You'll be combining all of the research you'll do within these chapters along with your own writing talent to produce material that reflects The Writer's Advantage.

THE CREAM RISES TO THE TOP

I have spent many years as a reader/story analyst and I can tell you that the percentage of material that stands out beyond the reader's stack is minimal. Know that the amount of average, mediocre material that is received by any media-related production entity is nearly 80–85% of their intake. It is rare that something new shows up and shines through, however it is always the case that the cream rises to the top. Your unique take on an already established genre will shine brilliantly — and you'll be able to defend it at every step along the way. Know this. Know that what you have to submit is probably as good — and definitely better when you follow the Genre Toolkit List's 10 steps — than a large percentage of what is being currently submitted.

WHY YOU?

When your material has moved up the ranks within the company, you'll eventually find yourself in the unique position of defending your work, and we'll discuss this process at length in Chapter 12. For now, however, this is where your thought process for defending your work begins.

First, continue to hold on to the reasons why you were originally attracted to your genre. Admiration is good. Admiration for a specific writer, book, TV series, or film, only fuels your own determination to produce material that is as good — or better. Nonetheless, your own understanding and admiration of your genre translates into your owning of that said genre. In other words, you know everything there is to know about romantic comedies. Those facts can only help you when you compose your own romantic comedy.

LACK OF CONFIDENCE

And so you say to yourself "Does the world really need another romantic comedy?" and you sabotage yourself because you tell yourself that you can't write a script like *When Harry Met Sally...* (1989) or *(500) Days of Summer* (2009), or a manuscript like *The Notebook* (2004). You become overwhelmed with a genre you know you love and you talk yourself out of it and you attempt to write something and then give up.

Writers are their own worse enemies. This method of sabotaging comes into play even before anything is written! And to this I say that I am so glad that Diablo Cody didn't talk herself out of writing *Juno* (2007). She herself refers to the piece as a "twisted love story" and at its base, it is a romantic comedy. She didn't lack the confidence to write this piece and she added her own unique style of dialogue and energy throughout. There are hundreds of examples like this. Think of one of your favorite books or movies. Imagine if the writer decided to give up because they thought no one would care or that there were enough of that type of book or film in the world.

Believe in your story. Build your confidence by doing the research. With each level and each chapter in this book, you'll gather information to support your work. You'll turn that information into knowledge for your idea and knowledge is power.

KNOW IT, OWN IT, MAKE THE GENRE BETTER

As you do this work, you'll not only build your confidence, you'll be able to fill in any loopholes when you do eventually defend your work. Because not only are you building upon your own pure and innocent enthusiasm, you are adding facts to your work. When a project comes across my desk, as I'm certain it is with most potential buyers, they want to work with the creator who is the most enthusiastic. Additionally, as you do this work, you'll be enriching your knowledge of the genre so you can intelligently make some changes within the genre. You will offer something new, or offer a game-changing element to the genre for your generation and for the future.

TOOLKIT SANDBOX

Some Questions and Your Fave Writer

QUESTIONING WITH THE WRITER'S ADVANTAGE

1. Who are your all-time favorite authors, showrunners, directors, writers from your youth?
2. What are your favorite books, TV shows, films from your youth?
3. What is your genre? Will you be working with a hybrid genre?
4. What will you bring to the genre that will be unique?
5. What is your special take on the genre? What do you bring to the table?
6. Why are you the one who should be writing this project?

7. Why should I buy your script or manuscript and not the next writer's who has written about the same subject matter?

EXERCISE

MY FAVORITE WRITER

Identify a favorite writer from your childhood/young adult history. Seek out information about their background and their influences. Chances are that you'll see a bit of the influencer's energy within their work. List five to ten elements that emerge from the work of the mentor into the mentee's work and describe why the protégé successfully took the mentor's work and made it their own.

CHAPTER 6

IDENTIFY YOUR GENRE'S QUINTESS-ENTIAL TEXT

You have identified your genre. Now dig in and continue with your research.

36 PLOTS

When writers say they have something new to pitch, something that has never been seen before, I'm always curious because that's a tall order to deliver. I find those writers are usually not aware of the 36 dramatic situations. According to most scholarly and literary sources, there are only 36 plots known to writers, so every genre you're working within has some prototypical text that is usually known universally as the exemplary classic text within the genre. Georges Polti, a French writer (1867–1946) is credited with identifying 36 dramatic situations within the writing universe. Some of these situations are: Madness, Disaster, Self-Sacrificing For An Ideal, Obstacles To Love, Ambition, Revolt, Pursuit, etc., and every storyline can be traced back to one of these — or a combination of these, depending on the complexity of the storyline in question — basic dramatic situations. Later, within the Questioning section of this chapter you'll be asked to locate the dramatic situation that best describes your project. This is fairly simple to identify. For instance, if you're writing a romantic comedy, most romantic comedies include the Obstacles To Love situation, or if you're writing a crime drama, you'll find Crime Punished By Vengeance or Crimes Of Love as the dramatic situations to choose from. Locate the dramatic situation that best describes your basic plot and by doing this exercise you'll further solidify your work within your chosen genre.

THE QUINTESSENTIAL TEXT

The next step is to locate the quintessential text within the genre. By this I mean locate the movie, TV show, book, or web series that would be considered to be the "granddaddy" of the genre. The quintessential text is the most perfect or typical example of that genre and is usually highly regarded and honored. Think *Star Wars* (1977) as the standard by which most science fiction adventure films are compared today, or *Bridget Jones's Diary* (1996 novel) for most contemporary chick lit franchises, *High Noon* (1952) for westerns, *Psycho* (1960) for psychological drama, *Citizen Kane* (1941) as a political drama, or *Dragnet* (1951–59, 1967–70) as the purest television police drama. Even though you may be writing a script, your quintessential text for your genre may have originally appeared in print or another form. All different types of media play into this research. Quintessential texts can be divided into sub-genres as well. For instance, *Caddyshack* (1980) is the quintessential text of all golfing-related comedies, and some might say *The Haunting of Hill House* (1959 novel) is the quintessential text of all paranormal psychological dramas, and *Night of the Living Dead* (1968) is the most influential movie of all zombie movies. Locating the quintessential text takes a bit of research as you may find a difference of opinion among critics/viewers/consumers regarding some of these titles due to generational and other differences, which we'll address later in this chapter. The identification of a specific title isn't always the end all and be all as you may find varying quintessential texts within your research. Having this information is part of The Writer's Advantage.

HOW TO FIND THE QUINTESSENTIAL TEXT

Begin by asking those around you — your peers, parents, children, friends, etc. — what their favorite movie, TV show, book, or web series is within your genre. Often parents can pass along favorite pieces of media from their generation to their children and children can do the same for their parents. In the case of many standard quintessential texts, it's because of familial information that has been passed down within generations that these pieces of popular culture are considered classics or standards beloved by many. If one generation says "You can't miss this!" — whatever "this" is — pay attention. You should listen to them. Whether you agree with them later, after you've read or viewed the text, is up to you. Having the knowledge of the text is what is key here.

After you've gathered the above recommendations, it's now time to begin with an internet and/or library search for your genre. Let's say you are writing a script that involves a road trip. When I do a search for "road trip movies" I discover links to articles such as "30 Great Road Trip Movies — *Entertainment Weekly*" and "20 Great 'Buddy' Road Trip Movies — Boston. com." When I peruse these sources I see a number of titles. None of the lists are exactly the same, and that's because of their source. Mainstream resources like *Entertainment Weekly* are going to represent a broader, general audience versus other resources that are cited. An established organization such as *The New York Times*, while also a mainstream source, will mention slightly different titles due to their specific audience needs, as will a site constructed by or for the fans of that particular genre. Pay attention to the source. There will be, however, titles that crossover and appear on all of these lists. Make it a point to know those titles.

Also, visit Wikipedia and search for your genre. In the case of "road trip movies," Wikipedia has them listed under "Road Movies" and further breaks them down according to style, topic, or setting, audience factors, and format/budgeting. Here you'll find more lists of road trip movies and again, once you have processed and honed in on the type of road movie you're writing, then compare this information to your other resources. In the case of road trip movies, some of the titles that appear on ALL of the lists (in no particular order) are *Easy Rider* (1969), *Sideways* (2004), *National Lampoon's Vacation* (1983), *Thelma & Louise* (1991), *The Motorcycle Diaries* (2004), *It Happened One Night* (1934), *Planes, Trains and Automobiles* (1987), *Lost In America* (1985), and *Midnight Run* (1988).

Next, make a note of the movies you've seen on this list and become acquainted with those you are not aware of by either reading about them and/or viewing them. You'd be surprised of how many times I have heard a pitch for a specific genre and the writer is not aware of an important text from their genre. For instance, a writer who pitches a romantic comedy and has never seen nor even heard of *Annie Hall* (1977) or *When Harry Met Sally...* (1987) — this has sadly happened I can tell you — does not make for a solid pitch. It is important that you know your genre — *everything* about your genre. And even if you have never SEEN *Annie Hall* or *When Harry Met Sally...* (which would put you at a disadvantage in pitching a rom-com), then at least state that you're aware of these movies. Not knowing about popular texts within your genre (and not just those from the immediate past/last five years) will result in you losing your pitch. I, as well as most producers, agents, and book editors, do not want to work with a writer who does not know their genre. That writer is clearly not writing with The Writer's Advantage.

Additionally, we live in a marvelous time where most of the websites we utilize as consumers automatically do our research for us. Every time you download a movie or TV show on Hulu or Netflix they automatically suggest a boatload of other titles under the genre you have just viewed. Amazon delivers this information with "Customers who bought this title also bought" and the "Frequently bought together" features to further assist you with your selections. For your purpose, however, you can study these titles and gain more information about your genre and your target audience. And of course you can search for film and TV shows on Amazon, so Amazon is often the best place to begin your search no matter what venue you are working within.

AN ABUNDANCE OF GENERATIONAL, ETHNIC, AND SUBJECTIVE DIFFERENCES

As you do this research you'll discover, as noted above, that different resources have slightly different lists and information about your genre. In most cases, this type of data changes according to generations, so it's important to note those movies or TV shows or books and even web series that are the oldest in their fields as they have stood the test of time. *This does not mean that they are the quintessential text, however, just because they are the oldest — they could be — but it is not the only requirement for a quintessential text.*

For instance, if we return to our list of well known, highly endeared road trip movies noted above, we see that the oldest title is *It Happened One Night* (1934). It's important that you're aware of this movie and because it continues to appear on various lists and critics and industry insiders continue to discuss it, there must be something about it that resonated to its original audience and continues to resonate to contemporary audiences. Make a note of this. In this case it's probably not the quintessential text of the entire genre, but it's important within the genre.

ROOM FOR DEBATE

Of the other titles — *Easy Rider, Sideways, National Lampoon's Vacation, Thelma & Louise, The Motorcycle Diaries, Planes, Trains and Automobiles, Lost In America,* and *Midnight Run* — there would be audiences and groups of fans who would debate that *Lost In America* is more of a road movie than *Easy Rider* and vice versa. Continue to do your research to determine what's being said about each (and all) of these movies. It's my guess that most would agree that *Easy Rider* is the quintessential road movie because in essence that is exactly (and only) what it's about — two guys heading out on the road in search of America. The movie appeared at a time in film history that reflected the zeitgeist of its audience and made a statement reflecting its generation and of youth in general. *Easy Rider* put this genre on the map (no pun intended).

The identification of quintessential texts can be mutable because different factors come into play; however, through this process of understanding what has been said about the movie in question and how the movie was received via box office receipts, cult/mainstream popularity, and collective memory, you should be able to determine one or two main movies within a genre that are important for you to pay attention to.

GAME CHANGERS

Additionally, you'll find that there are always important movies that introduce elements to the genre that become game changers within the genre. For example, *The Hunger Games* (2012) is a game changer in the action-adventure genre because it successfully features a female lead. Up until that point female action leads were few and far between and overall not taken seriously, only being seen as sexual objects. Often game changer texts are extremely important to study as they take the genre to another level, such as the *Harry Potter* franchise (1997–2007), which introduced a little wizard instead of the many little witches we knew in pop culture before that, or even a movie like *Ace Ventura: Pet Detective* (1994) — we have had hundreds of detective stories, but never a *pet* detective previous to this one. So you see how identifying a game changer in your genre is important.

SIFTING AND WINNOWING

As you examine the styles, the different settings and different time periods of your texts, along with their formats and level of popularity (by general and specific audiences), you'll be testing your own idea and comparing your idea to these classic (and not-so-classic) texts in your genre. At this point, you may find that the quintessential text for you leans towards one or another of the most endeared movies within your genre, and that's fine. You will ultimately use this title as the one that holds the highest standards for you. In the case of road movies, if your idea includes a young couple setting out to find their lives (or to find America or an answer of some sort), then *Lost In America* is a slightly better quintessential movie example for you than *Easy Rider*, which features two counter-cultural guys in search of existential dreams. They both have traits that you'll need and they both represent your genre, one is just a bit closer to your idea and therefore that's the one that becomes your quintessential text.

TOOLKIT SANDBOX

Twilight *Isn't the Only Game In Town, Some Questions, and Disaster-Rama*

CASE STUDY: VAMPIRE LITERATURE AND FINDING THE QUINTESSENTIAL TEXT

In vampire literature, research will unravel a "vampire craze" as far back as the 1720s and 1730s in Serbia. There's a short German poem entitled *The Vampire* (1748) by Heinrich August Ossenfelder where many of the traits we know of today — drinking of blood, living by night, preying upon virginal souls, etc. — unravel throughout. There's an obsession with these creatures during the 18th and 19th century throughout Eastern and Western Europe, although it isn't until the appearance of Bram Stoker's *Dracula* (1897), a novel, that the definitive description of the contemporary vampire we know appears. The name Count Dracula was inspired by a real person, Vlad Tepes ("Vlad the Impaler" is the original story upon which the vampire legend is based) who was a notorious Romanian prince in the 15th century. Author Stoker combines many of Tepes' modern-day myths that include blood-sucking creatures, a desire to live by night, the only way to kill them is through a stake in their heart, etc. — and this iconic figure is born.

If we skip ahead a few hundred years, we'll see the fact that one of our most popular vampire influences appears on television. *Dark Shadows* was an American TV series that appeared weekdays on ABC between 1966–1971. Gothic romance writer Marilyn Ross' franchise *Barnabas Collins* was the show's original text. As we learned in our brief history of mass media, there were only three television networks operating in the '60s. That fact plays into why *Dark Shadows* became so popular — it was the first vampire-related show on American television on a regular basis. Anyone between the ages of 6 and 66 who may have been interested in the occult or metaphysical stories watched this show with fanatical interest.

The show continued in syndication after its original run. It's a well-known fact that film directors Tim Burton and Quentin Tarantino were fans, along with Madonna and Johnny Depp. Depp vowed that he would one day play the lead Barnabas Collins and, in fact, Depp did indeed embody the character in the 2012 theatrical release which ultimately died (no pun intended) at the box office. That version of *Dark Shadows* will go down in history as an unauthentic text mostly due to the bastardization of the original storyline and a plot that had no direction whatsoever. View this version only after you have had the chance to see the original. You'll realize quickly why the Burton-Depp version sucked (flopped).

This *Dark Shadows* example illustrates how a piece of text that is well-known among a certain generation can rest quietly for a long time, only to be resurrected and celebrated once again, with a new spin for a new generation. *Dark Shadows* (2012) is an example of how a number of generations with curiosity in this text — along with those of a newer generation who have been exposed to vampires and all-things vampires via another source — mostly *Twilight* — can both enjoy a particular piece of popular culture, arriving at the text from different points of view.

Let's return to the 1970s, where *Dark Shadows* plays and a small, quiet group of folks gather as fans to watch (on weekdays no less!). At this same time, a series of novels by writer Anne Rice appears known as *The Vampire Chronicles*, with its first volume *Interview with the Vampire* (1976). The novel is a bestseller. Here the vampire legend lives on and has the opportunity to be interviewed (Rice's spin, her authentic version of this material) to tell us of his desires, his conquests, his history, etc. Readers are captivated and years later (1994) a filmed version is produced starring Tom Cruise and Brad Pitt and many would agree that the movie version would not be the quintessential text for the genre as the movie is a poor execution of the novel.

These texts influence writer Joss Whedon, who in 1992 writes a movie that becomes a popular television series (TV again) entitled *Buffy the Vampire Slayer*. Whedon incorporates postmodern and gender feminist theory into the vampire myth and an authentic text example is born (some might even say *Buffy* is a game changer as a female vampire is in the lead). With proper research, one would find many more popular books featuring the vampire legend, however it isn't until 2005 that Stephenie Meyer's series *Twilight* appears, and again a phenomenon occurs surrounding this genre. It seemed an entire new generation was waiting for their own vampire text, and they happily embraced Edward and Bella and the Pacific Northwest scenario these new vampires inhabited.

There have now been numerous additional vampire texts jumping on the *Twilight* bandwagon. There's *True Blood*, HBO's hugely successful vampire series, and *The Vampire Diaries,* another teen version of the vampire legend on the CW, created by Kevin Williamson and based on the books of the same name. Are these texts copycats of those listed above, or are they just examples of consistently good content? (The answer is they are consistently good content, as audiences are fascinated with the vampire legend — ever since the 1700s). Through all of these versions, research will show that Bram Stoker's *Dracula* is the quintessential text of the vampire genre.

It stands the test of time and features most, if not all, of the typical traits of vampire-related stories.

QUESTIONING WITH THE WRITER'S ADVANTAGE

1. Now that you've been introduced to the 36 dramatic situations, which one (or combination) best represents your plot? (There are any number of websites that will link you to the list of plots — just do a search for "36 dramatic situations" or Georges Polti.)

2. While doing your research, do authors of articles or web-based columns consistently refer to a specific title over and over and reference that title when comparing all titles within your genre? Make a note of this.

3. Within your research, is there a mention of a text that seemed to be a game changer for its genre? In other words, the movie, book, TV show, or web series that introduced something to the genre that forever changed the way that genre was made.

4. Continue to ask yourself, as you gather information and process the details, whether you agree with the critics and authors of articles, etc., with their choices for quintessential texts. Stand by your reasons and know why you do or do not concur with them.

5. Do you see the subjective evaluations that go into determining the quintessential texts for each genre due to generational, style, format, budget, and other factors?

6. Does your idea have the potential to be a game changer in your genre? Why?

7. Do you think a genre can exist without a quintessential text representing that genre?

EXERCISE

DISASTER-RAMA

Disaster movies of the 1970s provide a great scenario to study Quintessential Text energy. There have been many movies that feature disasters throughout the history of film, however the '70s are considered the Golden Age of disaster movies. Do some research on these movies. Hint: start with *Airport* (1970) and see where your research leads you. You'll see how an entire genre thrived off of one major movie hit.

CHAPTER 7

IDENTIFY THE TRAITS OF YOUR GENRE AND HOW THEY RELATE TO YOUR STORY

Every genre has its inherent traits. A trait is a characteristic, attribute, feature, property, mannerism, idiosyncrasy, peculiarity, quirk, and/or oddity that appears within that genre. These traits often solidify, hone, and make the genre what it is. It is the way these traits operate within any specific genre that make the genre unique. Think stranded, isolated, attractive teens and lots of partying in psychological horror movies, or gumshoe detectives and their final chances to prove themselves in murder mysteries, and moonstruck opposites that attract in romantic comedies, to name just a few examples of genre-specific traits.

HOW TO IDENTIFY TRAITS

In order to understand how to identify traits, let's dive into the vampire genre we explored in the last chapter. The first step is to gather and analyze the common characteristics of this genre and make a list. By doing this, you'll see how certain features and mannerisms consistently pop up within all vampire-related texts no matter what form they're in. These characteristics make up the genre. They are the ingredients that make the genre familiar. (In other words, these elements are the apples, sugar, flour, and maybe cinnamon that specifically make up the apple pie — otherwise, the apple pie would not be an apple pie, but some other kind of pie.)

The most common traits of vampire projects are (in no particular order):

Their vampire state cannot be cured or changed.
Vampires live by night and cannot be exposed to daylight (or it is difficult for them to be exposed to light).
They feed on the blood of other creatures and delight in human blood.
They are dead in the real sense, yet destined to roam the earth eternally for blood to exist.
They are predators, often in competition for the same blood sources.
They often "sleep" in coffins during the day, stay in abandoned buildings or castles.
They prey upon young, virginal, innocent souls.
They are thought of as evil; most humans want to avoid them.
Garlic cloves and religious crosses are often used to keep them away.
They can only be killed by a sword piercing their hearts.

This is by no means meant to be a complete list of traits of all vampire projects, however this list does begin to illustrate common elements that appear in most, if not all, vampire projects. We can do the same for zombies and werewolves and dragons, etc.

TRAITS THAT MORPH BETWEEN GENRES

If we continue in the same vein and begin to identify traits for zombies, for instance, we'll see that some of the traits crossover, or morph between the two genres, such as a desire to eat living animal and human flesh (instead of blood), and they are technically dead, however they never tire or run out of energy until they are destroyed, and their condition cannot be cured. As far as werewolves go, they too are addicted to blood, they are powerful creatures, and some say they can only be killed via a silver bullet (like a stake in the heart for vampires). I think you see a pattern emerging wherein specific traits make up specific genres. It would be rare to have a vampire desiring flesh and being destroyed by a silver bullet, just as animal and human blood is not enough for a zombie, as they need flesh in order to survive. You get it.

Taking a look at these specific characteristics will not only help you in solidifying your own work within your genre, but will also help you in selecting the traits you will utilize within your authentic text. Perhaps the morphing of some traits from one genre to another would result in a new, fresh way to execute the genre. Look at what Stephenie Meyer did with *Twilight*, adding the element of unrequited love to her vampire scenario. The opportunity is there for you to create a new level within your genre by first taking a look at what elements exist for you to work with within your genre sandbox.

CHARACTERS HAVE TRAITS TOO

Within your genre, character traits can be identified as well. These traits are usually applied to the main characters — e.g., most detectives and private eyes are usually single-widowed, divorced, never-married, etc.; you'd be hard-pressed to find a classic detective that was a well-established family man (or woman) and yes, the genre has emerged to include couples who sleuth together and they may or may not be romantically involved, but in the example of a single detective, that lead character is usually not family-friendly.

Since the 1990s, the rise of anti-heroes within television series has soared. Many would attribute this fact to the popularity of Tony Soprano of *The Sopranos* (1999–2007), a no-holds-barred type who killed, cheated, stole, lied, and suffered a breakdown all to the acceptance of the viewing public. So much so that many other "bad guy leads" have followed, such as serial killer Dexter Morgan in *Dexter* (2006–2013), meth dealer Walter White in *Breaking Bad* (2008–2013), womanizer/schmoozer Don Draper in *Mad Men* (2007–present), Tyrion Lannister in *Game of Thrones* (2011–present), Vic Mackey in *The Shield* (2002–2008), Nick Brody in *Homeland* (2011–present), and Stringer Bell in *The Wire* (2002–2008). All of these characters follow in Tony's lead, sometimes surpassing him with their immoral ways. You can make lists of characters' flaws (and attributes) and work with those elements also to continue to enhance your genre and the type of characters that inhabit your project.

"GOOD" TRAITS AND "BAD" TRAITS

As a genre goes through history, society and culture change and the genre grows along with its creators and consumers. Genres are fluid and mutable. That said, the genre must extend itself and grow along with the zeitgeist. It is your assignment as a writer to preserve the genre while at the same time introducing new ways to enjoy it.

There are times within this process that the introduction of a new way to write the genre is "good," meaning the authentic text resonates to and finds an audience. There are also times when new elements are introduced within a genre and the result is "bad," and they don't resonate to an audience and therefore the text is not entirely embraced by the public. The result is that sometimes the text is delegated to forever live on as only a cult favorite or forgotten completely. Let's look at two examples illustrating both of these outcomes.

"GOOD" TRAITS — THE SCREAM FRANCHISE

In 1996, screenwriter Kevin Williamson — a horror movie observer and fan — wrote his horror masterpiece *Scream*. Written in a weekend, *Scream* emphasized and called attention to the common devices and traits necessary within the horror genre. He identified all of them — attractive teenagers alone in a remote area, little or no electricity or power available to the helpless victims, use of everyday objects as murder weapons, surreal dream sequences that may or may not be happening in real-time within the film, absent parents, the typical oddball character who is probably not the murderer but then maybe he/she is, the little sister who does something wrong to entice the murderer, a murderer with a history of revenge for something horrible that happened to him in adolescence... and on and on. Williamson presented them anew within *Scream*. *Scream* lives not only within the horror genre, it is *about* the horror genre. Williamson successfully created a better horror film by incorporating the conventions that made the horror film genre popular. He wrote an authentic text within this already over-crowded and very popular genre.

A FAN OF MAD-SLASHER MOVIES

Williamson, like many others who grew up in the '70s and '80s, was very familiar with the three slasher film/psychological horror/horror franchises *Halloween* (1978–1995), *Friday the 13th* (1980–1993) and *Nightmare On Elm Street* (1984–1994).* These films became perennial favorites, very much a rite of passage

---

* *Halloween* and *Nightmare On Elm Street* featured films, novels, comic books, and TV shows during this time. Also, I am quoting only the films that appeared pre-1996, the time of Williamson's writing of Scream, because that is when the bulk of these films appeared on the scene. There have been additional films made in these franchises since 1996, however, they would not have influenced Williamson and his writing in 1996.

for most adolescents and very much a part of the pop culture. The effect of cable television in the '80s and '90s only added to the frenzy and popularity of each new addition to these franchises and fans consumed this material eagerly. Many of the creators of these slasher films would say that they were influenced by one pivotal fraternal mad-slasher film, the grand-daddy of them all, Alfred Hitchcock's *Psycho*, produced in 1960 (the quintessential text discussed in Chapter 6). This is one of the first rules of creating an authentic text — you'll usually be able to identify the seminal text that influences many others. *Psycho* influenced a generation of horror filmmakers and in turn that generation created a great deal of horror texts. It took one writer, however, to incorporate all of the devices of these texts into a new higher level and that was Kevin Williamson.

WHAT KEVIN WILLIAMSON DID

During the process of consuming *Scream* the viewer is exposed to the elements that make a horror film great. If one watched *Scream* and had never seen any of the original texts it was based upon — had never viewed a *Halloween* or *Elm Street* movie — they would still come away from the screening knowing what a horror movie was all about. Just like the processing of a parody, the audience laughs because they are familiar with the original content. Using the "good" traits within a text, the audience will come away from the experience knowing what the original content consisted of. They will perhaps learn something new, and/or be enlightened, inspired, surprised, etc. — there will be some element of gainful experience due to the consumption of this new version. This experience must be present in order to qualify a text as an authentic text that uses "good" traits within its composition. Some would also identify this as a post-modern twist on those mad slasher films.

Because a fresher version within the genre is created — a new spin on older, well-established conventions is made available. The genre then takes a leap and is re-created for a new audience, usually a new generation. But not always, and as we move quicker and faster through content, the generational differences will be less and less. The new audience will also embrace this new version — given they know the older versions and success is achieved. Williamson created an amazingly fresh new adaptation of old material, a hyper-version, so-to-speak. *Scream* is an example of an authentic text — it is a *very* good example of an authentic text.

"BAD" TRAITS — *THE CABIN IN THE WOODS* EXAMPLE

The use of certain traits that may not resonate with your audience, and taking a risk of introducing a trait to a genre that might not work can be illustrated through a continued discussion of the horror genre and the film *The Cabin In The Woods* (2012). This movie displays what happens when a writer/creator utilizes the same traits that a successful writer such as Williamson did — but fails.

With all due respect to horror expert Joss Whedon and his co-writer Drew Goddard, this film is referred to as "an astonishing meta-feat, capable of being funny, strange, and scary — frequently all at the same time" according to *rottentomatoes.com*, and there's often a mixed reaction from viewers who have seen the film. Yes, those same basic "scary movie" traits are present — there are five friends/students in a remote cabin, no one seems to know they are there, lots of sex and booze and pot are anticipated, yet there's a strange and ominous presence that keeps the party from getting truly started.

Some reviews state that this movie takes the post-modern twist and twists that hook even harder. The twist here (SPOILER ALERT) is the presence of technicians working in a hidden underground facility who are conducting a mysterious ritual of some sort — a game in progress. Framing the same plot within a reality show scenario is a new trait that is introduced to this genre. Additionally, when one of the five students discovers wires within their rustic cabin, the plot shifts and many would say that this is where the film sabotages itself.

What follows are the same gruesome deaths as seen within all mad slasher movies, leaving two survivors, however these survivors infiltrate the facility where the technicians are manipulating the game along with a cache of monsters and items that usually invoke fear in humans. While offering a great display of visual delights, the plot continues to veer so far away from the original storyline that some might find the film to be laughable. The two survivors and the audience learn that a group known as the "Ancient Ones" who lie in slumber as these "games" or rituals are being conducted await the final victim — the virgin — to be killed to complete the ritual. During this very-difficult-to-watch revealing of the overall plot, even veteran actress Sigourney Weaver's appearance can't save this storyline from drowning within its own overwritten plot.

Whedon himself has explained that this movie is an example of the de-evolution of the horror film genre. The film received many positive critical reviews and found a cult following among a certain faction of horror film fanatics, however the introduction of the "reality show" framing and outrageous conceptual ending around the usual plot did not help this genre move to a new, authentic level.

Overall, this is an example of the risk that can take place when introducing new traits along with the genre's traditional traits.

This is not to say that taking risks always results in a cult-only audience following. The entire reason for exploring usual traits of a genre is to experiment and branch out to eventually reach an authentic text written by you.

TOOLKIT SANDBOX

Non-Utopian Worlds, Some Questions, and Some Fish-Out-Of-Water Stories

CASE STUDY: KNOW YOUR TRAITS IN DYSTOPIAN LITERATURE

Novels that incorporate tried and true traits within their genre often coincide with content that becomes wildly popular with their consumers. In the case of *The Hunger Games* by Suzanne Collins, this fact is true. Collins' trilogy incorporates traits seen in many other Young Adult and Literary Fiction titles that explore dystopian themes. The author herself credits getting her idea after watching competition-based reality shows and footage from the invasion of Iraq, which is often described as a post-apocalyptic landscape. By combining these two elements she created a dystopian environment where Katniss Everdeen, a 16-year-old lead female is our guide while teenagers fight to stay alive in an arena of ultimate competition.

The Hunger Games trilogy is a perfect example of the genre of dystopian literature that utilizes all the basic traits of this genre. Some of these traits are: extreme odds to beat to stay alive for everyone left alive, a tragic environment where survival is the primary task on hand for the characters, extreme youth and/or old age are the only segments of the population, fear of mass plagues persists, all forms of terrorism seem to permeate the population, and the bleak hope for the future always seems to remain just one step ahead of the hero, yet he/she continues to strive toward that saving grace — that survival mechanism, whatever it is.

That said, previous pieces of beloved literature such as *Fahrenheit 451* (1953) by Ray Bradbury and *1984* (1949) by George Orwell both feature lead characters who take drastic steps to challenge the way their government conspiracy-based worlds filled with mind control and revolution are operated. One could look to aspects of Ayn Rand's *Anthem* (1938) and *Atlas Shrugged* (1957), Aldous Huxley's *Brave New World* (1932), and Margaret Atwood's *A Handmaid's Tail* (1985) to view lead characters that found loopholes in their controlled societies to achieve freedom.

But it is in the 1954 novel *The Lord of the Flies* by William Golding that the *Hunger Games* franchise finds a true predecessor, and this is mostly because of the teenage boys who find themselves stranded on a deserted island without adults where they need to construct a government and way of life alone. This book raises many questions about basic human behavior and pits the boys against each other — very similar in scenario to Suzanne Collins' fictional world. And so, within all of these classic, time-tested previous novels there are the many traits that can be found threaded within them. Whether intentional or coincidental, Collins took aspects of other well-known novels and utilized them within her trilogy to produce a game-changing franchise (as discussed in Chapter 6) for not only Young Adult readers, but all fiction lovers at the same time. She succeeded in creating an authentic version of the dystopian literature novel. This is an example of a writer displaying The Writer's Advantage, not only because she was able to produce a higher level version of a genre, but was also able to find a way for the content to resonate to her current audience. She made some major changes, including a strong female lead and extremely violent scenes involving teens killing teens, however she stayed within the genre's lines and utilized the genre's traits to take the genre to the next level. Now it is up to the next writer of Young Adult dystopian novels to produce their own authentic version of *The Hunger Games*. Many have identified *Divergent* (2011 novel) to have followed in Collins' footsteps. What traits will your version include?

QUESTIONING WITH THE WRITER'S ADVANTAGE

1. As you gather the traits inherent to your genre and/or characters, what are the most essential ones?
2. Are you attracted to your genre because of the traits of the genre?
3. Are you able to identify how traits have evolved and perhaps merged within your genre?
4. What are the genre's traits that you will use within your authentic text?
5. What are the genre's traits you do not want to use or will not emphasize within your authentic text?
6. Do you recognize how you will utilize the genre's basic traits in your authentic text?
7. Are you going to introduce new traits to the genre within your authentic text?

EXERCISE

FISH-OUT-OF-WATER STORIES

Identify the traits of fish-out-of-water television series, everything from the iconic *Beverly Hillbillies* (1962–1971) as Texas hillbillies find their way in Beverly Hills, to New Mexico-to-NYC law officer *McCloud* (1970–1977), to a cousin from another country in *Perfect Strangers* (1986–1993), to aliens vs. earthlings in *3rd Rock From the Sun* (1996–2001) and to rich kids versus poor kids in *The O.C.* (2003–2007). As you identify the reoccurring traits, also note how those traits evolve throughout the decades and from comedy to drama and genre to genre.

CHAPTER 8

IDENTIFY THE MASS PRODUCTION HISTORY OF YOUR GENRE

You have your quintessential text. You have your list of traits. Now let's look at how history has treated your genre. Your research will take you down many paths as you'll learn how books within your genre have been adapted into films and television series and some films and series are adapted into print — and why. This research assists you in knowing where you would best find an audience for what you've created.

RUN THE HISTORY

Take your genre and run the history of the genre. In other words, check at least three sources that confirm the definition of the genre and examples of said genre in contemporary media over the last 30 to 50 years (earlier if you wish). It would be time-consuming to watch every text within the history of your genre. A shortcut would be to go back to the highlighted texts you found for the quintessential text research in Chapter 6.

For the sake of illustrating how to go about this search, let's say that I have written a bible for a cop/detective drama series and

I want to apply the work of *The Writer's Advantage* before I begin shopping the project. I'm going to use the genre of cop/detective shows and run through the highlights of this genre in contemporary television history. You'll see that we will incorporate our quintessential text element, along with the traits of the genre, as we analyze how the genre has been played out on television over the years.

During television's early years, the cop/detective drama genre found an audience mostly due to the gumshoe detective stories heard on the radio previously and found in pulp fiction novels and *film noir* movies of the 1930s and '40s. Sam Spade, the lead P.I. of the *film noir* movie classic *The Maltese Falcon* (1941), was perhaps the most well-known detective of that era. *The Maltese Falcon* itself originally appeared as a novel in 1930, written by Dashiell Hammett, and over the years had been adapted numerous times for film. And so, in the 1950s, when television was a new medium, there were many readers/viewers willing to invite these TV sleuths into their living rooms on a weekly basis.

Dragnet (1951–1959, 1967–1970), featuring Jack Webb as Sgt. Joe Friday, was at first a radio series, then a television series, and eventually a movie (1987). Some might say that *Dragnet* in all of its forms is a quintessential text for this genre. The scripted show featured cases from real-life scenarios set in Los Angeles. The anxieties of the times shined through. For instance, the cops held a straight-laced law-and-order mentality when it came to the delinquent teenagers using/selling drugs and the rough-and-dirty bad guys. The youths were either set straight or taught a lesson (crime doesn't pay). *Dragnet* found a loyal audience. Another cop-message show that played out as a junior *Dragnet* was *Adam-12* (1968–1975). This early police procedural ran beyond the run of the original *Dragnet* and found the two lead cops dealing with more scandalous issues.

The storylines became grittier. We'll see that this is a characteristic of cop/detective shows as they mirror their places in time.

Hill Street Blues (1981–1987) featured the Hill Street station in a nondescript city that served as the front lines of the chaos at bay that was going to destroy society. These stories, often two or three plots intertwined within one episode, reflected the worry of society about whether the world was going down the drain because of uncontrolled and exponential crime. *NYPD Blue* (1993–2005) offered a message of social redemption and fairness during the '90s, when the mood to feel good about ourselves and live worry-free after the Cold War ended translated into detectives always catching their villain and acting compassionately. By the '00s, *The Wire* (2002–2008) brilliantly gave us the message that after decades of losing the war on drugs and failing in attempts to improve education, the situation was hopeless. Our social institutions, such as the police department and schools, had become twisted into dysfunction beyond all hope of salvation (just as society had been doing in the '00s in real life). By looking at just five series from 1951 to 2008 we see a progression of realism that reflects the culture they played within and to.

We have since seen the realism element taken to even deeper levels with the *Law & Order* (1990–2010) and *NCIS* (2003–present) police procedural drama series (to name just two of many) continuing to write weekly plots that feature storylines direct from current headlines. Along with those plots, violent, bloody visuals peppered with offensive language and sexual situations permeate this genre. As you view your genre going through its history, notice how basic elements within their storylines are treated at each step and make note of this.

Next, after analyzing the style and execution of these shows, take a look at how the traits have been utilized. In the case of cop/detective shows, there is a strong emphasis on loyalty. The type of loyalty can vary, such as to one's partner, to the squad, to the "job" as an institution, or to society at large. This loyalty works for both sides. The criminals, particularly gang members, never expose fellow members. The truth is another trait. All cop shows play with the meaning of "the truth" in various contexts — such as the truth of knowing someone is guilty but not being able to prove it, the truth as expressed in court by evidence, the truth twisted or ignored in interrogations, covering up the truth to sidestep institutional dysfunction and achieve some noble end, and the personal impact on officers' lives when the truth is covered up, or conversely when some dark secret is revealed.

Remember when we said that characters also have traits (Chapter 6)? Cop/detective shows are classic examples of this. Police are real, complex characters who are flawed in some way. Lead P.I. *Columbo* (1971–2003) wore a rumpled raincoat, smoked a cigar, and bumbled his way (usually knowing exactly what he was doing) through his murder-solving cases. *Kojak* (1973–1978) featured a bald detective with an attitude who always had a Tootsie Pop in his mouth and muttered the catchphrase "Who loves ya baby?" *Barney Miller* (1974–1982), a rare cop comedy, featured a collection of oddball cops inhabiting a Greenwich Village police station. Iconic cops such as Andy Sipowitz in *NYPD Blue* and Adrian Monk in *Monk* (2002–2009) embody the type of civil servant who excels at his work no matter what. Additionally, these main series characters often struggle with real-life issues. Alcoholism and family problems are a common symptom of the rough lives that cops and detectives lead. It seems alcoholism is accepted among the police more than it might be in other professions and almost excused because of the nature of the job. Identifying these traits within highlighted texts assists you as you gather information for your own project(s) on hand.

Through this very brief search you can see the evolution of this genre and how the genre changed through time, and if I introduce a show like *Dexter* (2006–2014) into this mix, you can see how the genre has, in fact, moved from being a one-sided "good guys vs. bad guys" scenario into a situation where a real "bad guy," a serial killer, is working within and employed by the Miami police department. Where will this genre go next? That's up to you as you gather this information.

Also note that I could also include in my search all of the cops and detectives found in literature and in films even though I am working with a television series. I would suggest going about doing this chronologically within each medium and then look at all of the information you've gathered before perfecting your own material. Arm yourself with as much knowledge about your genre as possible.

HYBRID GENRES

We have reviewed (in Chapter 5), how genres can be combined and the recent trend of merging genres into hybrids of genres. Also, establishing new sub-genres is on the rise.

Hybrid genres play to crossover audiences and within different platforms of the transmedia universe and the result can be very lucrative. Take a look at the *Dexter* example previously mentioned. The series has attracted viewers interested in police procedurals along with those interested in psychological horror. Combining two successful genres is often a win-win situation. There is no end to how genres can be combined. The opportunities are wide open and there are no rules.

Let's take a look at the Dark Fantasy genre within the publishing world. This genre is the combination of horror and fantasy. Texts such as Stephen King's *The Dark Tower* series (1982–2012) or Raymond Feist's *Faerie Tale* (1988) fall into this category. The Dark Fantasy genre also runs the gamut of gothic fiction, horror fiction, occult detective, supernatural fiction, sword and sorcery, urban fantasy, and weird fiction, and carries over into the filmed and digital adaptations of the content within this genre.

As a creator of a hybrid genre it is beneficial for you to know both (or more) genres well. Remember that you will be attracting audiences from all of your genres and you do not want to disappoint half (or a third, etc.) of your audience. Therefore, if you do work with a hybrid genre, the research you'll be conducting will be for all the genres combined.

MANUSCRIPTS VS. SCRIPTS

As you conduct this research, observe the way the material first appeared on the scene, be it in print, on the radio, within the early television scenario, or via the large screen (in theaters) or small screen (via computers and mobile applications). It all boils down to content, no matter what the original venue is and making note of how, for instance, previously mentioned *Dragnet* transferred from radio to television to film will only enhance your chances of knowing how best to present your own material. In today's market the options of writing a manuscript versus a script prevail. There are benefits to writing each.

My experience has been that in most cases, it is difficult for a novelist to write scripts and equally as frustrating for a screenwriter to write prose. The formats differ greatly and the discipline involved in writing each require mastering the unique format required.

Within screenwriting the "economic use of words" takes over. Within prose writing, the writer is free to write lavish description and narrative without any restraints. In other words, a novelist could take a complete page to describe a memorable, significant sunset within their plot, while a screenwriter must use only one word — SUNSET.

There are very few truly talented writers who can write successfully in each discipline and flourish. I would advise most writers to choose the venue they wish to write within and stick with it. The only time that you may consider writing the "other" version of a script would be if a producer or development exec asks you to, or mentions that they'd like to see the material fleshed out in novel form. The reason for this is that they may not be able to see the scope of your idea within a 110-page script. If you flesh out your story completely through prose, additional subplots and characters will emerge and the overall effect makes the project bigger and more appealing to the potential buyer.

On the other hand, if you have written a manuscript and submit it and the potential buyer asks you to adapt the material into script form, that is when you need to ask if they are seriously interested in buying the material. Do not, under any circumstances, adapt your manuscript to script form without a deal (option or buy-out) in place. Most writers will receive an additional fee (in some cases quite large), to write the script version of their material. Do not work for free in this case.

If you wish to write both a prose and script version of your content before you begin shopping your material, that is completely up to you. Many writers have done this. This option gives you a higher chance at getting picked up by either the publishing world or the entertainment industry when you shop your content within both arenas. When one or the other expresses interest and buys your work, you'll already have the additional adaptation ready. But don't give it away, make sure your agent negotiates a deal when it comes time to writing the adaptation (script) or additional material (manuscript). Then present that "new" version in a reasonable amount of time and receive payment for your hard work.

So if you feel you would like to market and shop within both the publishing world and the entertainment industry, then it would behoove you to write both versions. You increase your chances of selling your project.

TOOLKIT SANDBOX

Steampunk'd, Some Questions and Westerns, What a Great Combination

CASE STUDY: STEAMPUNK'D

"Steampunk" is primarily a literary genre, a sub-genre of Science Fiction and a hybrid of Sci-Fi, Historical, and Fantasy. These works are alternative worlds that parallel the 19th century British Victorian era or the American Wild West in a post-apocalyptic/fantasy future where steam power is once again in fashion. The style of Jules Verne, H. G. Wells and Mary Shelley is copied here and the genre looks to Fritz Lang's movie *Metropolis* (1927) as its quintessential text, along with H. G. Wells' novel *The Time Machine* (1895) as a close runner-up. In this case, this cross-genre, even though it is embedded in history, isn't identified until the late 1980s in America as a genre that would stand parallel alongside Cyberpunk. One of the best primary texts of this genre is the television show *The Wild Wild West* (1965–1969). Here's an example of how the networks took on a series as competition to the spy dramas — *The Man From U.N.C.L.E* (1964--1968), *The Avengers* (1961–1969), *Get Smart* (1965–1970) — that were hugely popular in the '60s, along with the James Bond films playing in the theaters, and combined them with the television westerns — *Bonanza* (1959–1973), *Gunsmoke* (1955–1975), *The Big Valley* (1965–1969) — that were just about wearing out their welcome with American television audiences. The result was *The Wild Wild West*, featuring two secret service agents working within the backdrop of the American West and utilizing technologically advanced devices to fend off their villains. Brilliant idea for the '60s, so brilliant that two television movies were produced with the original cast in 1979 and 1980, and a movie version exists from 1999 starring Will Smith. Watching how this genre shined in the '60s and slowly fell by the wayside in its subsequent versions (mostly due to the lack of interest among audiences — both spy dramas and westerns had played themselves out within the television landscape, leaving the original idea with much to be desired by 1999, the end of the 20th century) is a lesson to be learned regarding how genres resonate to specific audiences during specific time periods.

There are two more movie projects that exhibit Steampunk energy and have garnered significant followings. *The League of Extraordinary Gentlemen* (1999 graphic series, 2003 film adaptation) and *Sherlock Holmes* (2010) each gracefully embrace all of the traits and elements of pure Steampunk. On television, *The Adventures of Brisco County, Jr.* (1993–1994) had a short run on the CW network. The show had a small but dedicated following, although not enough to be renewed for a second season.

As mentioned in the beginning of this chapter, this is a fairly new hybrid genre. It is, for the most part, untested and could either explode in popularity or move into pure cult status depending on where creators want to take it. In this case study, we've discovered a fairly new genre that holds much potential. Its elements are specialized, representing a niche of one popular genre — Sci-Fi — and one not-so-popular genre, the

Western. Care to explore any more and move forward with your own version of the next big Steampunk property?

QUESTIONING WITH THE WRITER'S ADVANTAGE

1. How have the print, film, television, and web-based versions of your genre fare among audiences through the decades?

2. Do you see a pattern emerge from your genre throughout the shifts within the genre?

3. Did society and cultural influences help or hinder your genre throughout the ages?

4. Did generational shifts play a part in how/why your genre did particularly well — or not?

5. Does your genre hold up over time — why?

6. Does your genre hold up over time — why not?

7. Do you have a hybrid or cross-genre in mind?

EXERCISE

GO WEST

Westerns have not stood the test of time, especially within the 21st century. Study this genre to understand why some genres shine consistently and others fade away. (Hint: The entertainment powers that be have attempted cross-genre versions of westerns to drum up appeal for this genre pay extra-special attention to these pieces of content, such as 2011's *Cowboys & Aliens*.)

CHAPTER 9

ANALYZE AUDIENCE REACTION — MASS OR CULT?

To help you in honing and defining your idea to ensure that it will resonate with your audience, you took a look at the history of your genre in Chapter 8. Now it is time to take another, deeper step into the genre and study why some texts become wildly popular and are thought of as mainstream, and others reach a more limited cult status. In order to best measure the popularity of a genre, one has to look at 1.) the social and political backdrop at the time of release/distribution, and 2.) the media measuring devices in place during the time of consumption, either initially or during the text's long tail of consumption.

In regard to pre-20th century texts that appeared originally in newspapers, magazines, and/or as books, one must gather material that is available through print-related accounts only. Upon looking at pieces of popular culture from the 1920s through current times, it is possible to find measures specific to each type of media, such as *The New York Times* bestselling books lists, box office receipts for movies, and ratings for television fare. Within the 21st century, the number of hits per video or webisode and the number of tweets surrounding a specific piece of media is the measure of popularity. Understanding how the text was received when it first appeared on the scene and later how it is remembered is also something to take into consideration. For instance, films such as *The Rocky Horror Picture Show* (1975) and *Harold and Maude* (1971) are considered cult classics, but so is *The Room* (2003). Economic, historical, and social factors play into why a text may or may not play well when it first appears on the scene and what its performance level may eventually reach after its initial release. So let's look at the definition of mainstream versus cult and why some texts resonate and others don't.

MAINSTREAM OR CULT

By mainstream I mean acceptance within popular culture; in other words, the general consensus among consumers — the large group of individuals who viewed the movie, read the book, accessed the web series, etc., found the text to be interesting, entertaining, and worthy of their time. The opposite of this scenario are texts that find themselves liked only by cult followings — specific alternative groups within society that include subcultures and countercultures.

In most cases, writers write their material in the hope of achieving commercial and financial success, and there are some writers who may not be that concerned with commercial success but write to bring awareness to an issue or to reveal the truth about a specific topic. You have no control over how audiences are going to consume and react to your work, no matter what your original intention is for the work in question.

So, why do some texts become favorites within pop culture and others continue to be perpetuated throughout time? Sometimes the answer goes back to the traits found in most texts.

We can look at movies, TV shows, books, and study all of the "best of" lists, but mostly it takes looking at each text and how and where it was released and the journey the text took to find its audience. Some of our classic films such as *The Wizard of Oz* (1939) and *Citizen Kane* (1941) did not open to great box office receipts, yet, through word of mouth and critical acclaim, they have become important movies that reflect American culture and have found their place in mainstream film history. There are also films such as *The Sound of Music* (1965) that did enjoy box office success when first released and continues to appear on most "best of" lists. It seems this film is loved by many and has been passed down from generation to generation. Its themes of love, family values, religious versus secular pursuits, persecution — all set to memorable music — never seem to tire. The film plays annually on American network television and appears as a sing-a-long musical at special screenings across the country. Its release in 1965 was against the social challenges that America faced at the time — racism, violence, economic uncertainty, counter-culture threats from "hippies" and Vietnam protestors. Is that why the film did so well? It was an escape from the reality facing the American public. This is a mainstream text.

As far as cult films, the two mentioned above, *The Rocky Horror Picture Show* and *Harold and Maude*, did not receive box office love when first released. So what contributed to their long lasting achievement as cult favorites? In their case they both appeared in the '70s and the traditional movie release pattern was in place (as explained in Chapter 1). In the mid-to-late '70s, urban theaters that had been left behind for suburban movieplexes began showing foreign films and "midnight movies." *Pink Flamingos* (1972) and *Reefer Madness* (1936) were being shown at midnight in New York City. On April Fools Day, 1976, *Rocky Horror* followed in their steps.

The Rocky Horror Picture Show became the midnight destination in many urban areas (230 theaters across the country), and not only would you attend the showing, you would also dress up as one of the many characters who inhabit the haunted mansion that lead characters Brad and Janet stumble upon. Props, sing-a-longs, and dancing took place at every screening, and as each week went by, the audiences grew and grew. *Harold and Maude*, essentially a love story, followed in the midnight screening time slot. Attending one of these screenings in the late '70s meant mouthing along with the audience as they recited many of Harold's famous lines regarding his suicide attempts and singing along with the Cat Stevens soundtrack.

You can still find screenings of these films in urban movie houses, despite their ready availability for home viewing.

Both are important movies to view to understand how cult films find their audience.

AND SPEAKING OF LISTS

Throughout the year various organizations present their "Top 10 Best" lists — the 10 best books, the 10 best movies, the 10 best TV shows, etc., of the year, or the "Top 25" or "Top 100 Best" lists of all time, etc. No matter whether these lists are being generated by major newspapers or fan-based websites, the general public has a fascination with categorizing pieces of media. These lists are composed by critics, fans, consumers, and media experts and companies. A particular text appears within the list and it appears there for a reason, as a majority of individuals think it should be there based on some level of popularity. (Many of these are the same lists referred to in Chapter 6 and often include the quintessential text for your research).

Mainstream magazine *Entertainment Weekly* loves to produce these lists. For instance, here is their list for the 10 Greatest American Sitcoms from their July 5/12, 2013, "The 100 All-Time Greatest Movies...and TV Shows...and Albums...and Novels... and More" issue:

The Simpsons (1989–present)
Seinfeld (1990–1998)
The Mary Tyler Moore Show (1970–77)
All In The Family (1971–79)
The Andy Griffith Show (1960–68)
I Love Lucy (1951–57)
Cheers (1982–93)
The Cosby Show (1984–92)
Roseanne (1988–97)
Arrested Development (2003–06, 2013)

The list spans six decades (1951–2013), and+ if we return to our discussion from Chapter 1 and the way media played to an unfragmented audience during that time, these shows achieved success because the majority of Americans watched them on television in real-time and via taped and DVR episodes. The masses enjoyed these shows and continue to discuss these shows. Writers who grew up consuming these shows are still in many of the writers' rooms of shows being produced today. As creators and consumers we have embraced these shows as most of them revolve around relatable family and social issues. If you run through the traits of each of these sitcoms you'll find many of them to be similar, such as family values, family dysfunction, friendships, comedic scenarios, gender issues, and comments on society (especially within *Seinfeld* and *The Simpsons*). There are common threads that tie each of these shows together as each one appears from decade to decade. If you want to appeal to the masses, take a look at these Top 10 lists and identify what appears in each of the shows and then apply those same traits to your material.

In the case of cult followings, let's take a look at two more lists from the same issue:

10 Greatest Dramas	10 Greatest Cult Classics
The Wire (2002–08)	*The Wire* (2002–08)
The Sopranos (1999–2007)	*Buffy The Vampire Slayer* (1997–2003)
Buffy The Vampire Slayer (1997–2003)	*Arrested Development* (2003–06, 2013)
Mad Men (2007–2014)	*My So-Called Life* (1994–1995)
Breaking Bad (2008–2013)	*The X-Files* (1993–2002)
My So-Called Life (1994–1995)	*Doctor Who* (1963–present)
Law & Order (1990–2010)	*Star Trek: The Next Generation* (1987–94)
Lost (2004–10)	*Mystery Science Theater 3000* (1988–99)
Prime Suspect U.K. (1991–2006)	*The Comeback* (2005)
The X-Files (1993–2002)	*It's Always Sunny in Philadelphia* (2005–present)

First, within the Dramas list we see similar traits among the shows again, such as compelling storylines, strong lead characters, captivating seasonal arcs, a preponderance of anti-heroes. Next, the texts mentioned are fairly recent within the history of media, all from the '90s, '00s, through to the present except for *Doctor Who*, which goes back to 1963. First, take a look at that fact and that most of the critics and experts that gathered these lists only really truly remember the last 10 to 20 years of content.

As for cult followings, 4 of these 20 series selections appear on both lists. This proves that there can be a fine line between mainstream and cult content. In the case of *The Wire*, *Buffy The Vampire Slayer*, *My So-Called Life*, and *The X-Files*, there are enough viewers within mainstream media who find these shows to be of interest and there are cult fans who continue to perpetuate the series content beyond the series' time and place in television history.

My So-Called Life is an interesting selection, as it was only broadcast for one season. There are only 19 episodes, yet, due to the fact that the show originally ran on network television, ABC, it also received a run on MTV and other networks on a syndicated basis and continued to pick up audiences every time it was shown. The series features issues of adolescent angst — something that everyone can relate to — and due to that fact, just about anyone who views the difficult life of teenager Angela Chase gets sucked into understanding everything she goes through. It is a classic series, as it could have appeared at any time in television history.

As far as the other cult classics, they differ in genre — sci-fi, comedy, drama — yet each one has somewhat quirky elements, from dealing with aliens and vampires to Lisa Kudrow's *The Comeback*, a brilliantly written show about the struggles of being a forthysomething actress in Hollywood that appeared for only one season on HBO. Here's an example of a well-written show that didn't reach its audience during its initial run, but has since rounded up a great deal of praise and enthusiasm from those who discover it. This is the future of media. We will see more and more of these small, quiet shows find an audience as Netflix and Amazon continue with their unique distribution.

So what does that mean for you as a writer in this marketplace? It means that you have the opportunity to write for mainstream, niche, cult, or any combination of these types of audiences.

It means that you can intend for a specific group of consumers to enjoy your work, but you'll never know what group will gravitate to your work until your work is released.

TOOLKIT SANDBOX

De Palma's Obsession, Some Questions, and The Room

CASE STUDY: BRIAN DE PALMA AND HIS OBSESSION WITH HITCHCOCK

Whatever you think of the work of Brian De Palma, you have to give him credit for wearing his admiration for Alfred Hitchcock on his sleeve. With any study of De Palma's work you will inevitably find a writer, critic, or author discussing how De Palma consistently copies (some would say rips off) Hitchcock's scenes within his movies, from *Obsession* (1976) to *Femme Fatale* (2002), but most especially in the back-to-back sexual thrillers *Dressed to Kill* (1980), *Blow Out* (1981), and *Body Double* (1984).

This triad of movies featured grisly mysterious murders, dark surroundings, violence in public places, *Psycho*-like shower scenes, double identities, surprise twists, shapeshifter characters, etc., culminating in many critics out and out stating that *Body Double* was just simply a literal remake of Hitchcock's *Rear Window* (1954).

So how does the director of such popular mainstream films as *Carrie* (1976), *Scarface* (1983), and *The Untouchables* (1987) fall into a cult-level status as a result of too closely copying

Hitchcock, THE master of suspense? How did these homages to a fellow director go awry for De Palma?

I'm sure De Palma's intentions were good. Obviously, he is influenced by one of the great directors, as we are all influenced by our mentors. He grew up watching Hitchcock's films and wanted to emulate them, this is clear. However, when similar elements are executed (no pun intended) by De Palma, the result is either so incredibly unbelievable or cheesy that we can't take him seriously. The result is that *Dressed to Kill*, *Blow Out*, and *Body Double* have achieved cult status — for all the wrong reasons. Some viewers love these films, mostly because they can see what De Palma was *trying* to do. It's a noble attempt, however the results drew criticism. Take some time to view these three films (only after you have watched your necessary Hitchcock films first, such as *Psycho*, *Strangers on a Train*, *North by Northwest*, *Vertigo* — at least), and you'll see how one director's "homage" perhaps goes too far. Does De Palma's admiration pay off? I'll let you be the judge.

Learn from this. If you are going to include references to writers, directors, producers who have preceded you, at least do them well. (For an opposing look at how one director successfully applies homage to cinematic predecessors, study the films of Quentin Tarantino. He has mastered the homage factor, no doubt.)

QUESTIONING WITH THE WRITER'S ADVANTAGE:

1. As you do your research, ask yourself "How do I anticipate my project being accepted by audiences?"
2. Would your audience consider your work to be mainstream? Why?
3. Would your audience consider your work to be a candidate for a cult favorite? Why?

4. Are you considering all types of consumers as potential audiences?
5. What are your favorite cult movies, TV shows, books? Why?
6. Do you think some individuals like unusual (not mainstream) movies because they want to appear to be different?
7. If you like cult material, does that make you odd? Do you think differently of folks who like material that is not usually considered mainstream?

EXERCISE

INSIDE *THE ROOM*

Identify some films from the past two decades that have achieved cult status (include Tommy Wiseau's *The Room*). Why are they considered cult films? Why didn't they reach the mainstream audience?

TRENDS AND PATTERNS OF YOUR GENRE

As you continue to research your genre, you'll need to examine how the texts you've been studying build off of one another. This is not only identifying and understanding the influences of a particular writer, but also being aware of how all of these creators of content have come together to write similar themes and ideas within genres. Studying how writers pay homage to existing texts to build their own texts is important. This produces patterns within a genre that lead to trends within that genre.

NOBODY KNOWS ANYTHING

In 1983 novelist/screenwriter William Goldman wrote a quintessential book about writing in Hollywood entitled *Adventures in the Screen Trade*. (You should read it, no matter what kind of writer you are.) In it he stated that "Nobody knows anything" when it comes to studios and networks as they put together their rosters for the next blockbuster summer season or television season. And this remains true to this day. Yes, there is a massive amount of research conducted and Twitter responses are monitored, however, what ultimately happens at the box office on any given weekend or when a new TV series is broadcast or available via a web service, the distributors (along with the creators of the content) do not really know whether the pieces of content will be a hit or a miss.

The reason I am bringing this up at this point is that sometimes there's this mysterious thing that happens among development folks, and often they end up developing similar projects — at random. Sometimes this has to do with the culture, as an issue is going on in society (such as fear of infectious disease or terrorism hijinks) and development executives pick up on that, or it has to do with the zeitgeist that we all live in and the patterns of the everyday lives we lead. When you study Joseph Campbell and his discussion about myths, and later work with Christopher Vogler's *The Writer's Journey*, you'll understand that our media is just a reflection of the collective consciousness of our times, and movies (and content within all media in general) are our modern-day contemporary myths. Being aware of this and knowing how to tap into that collective consciousness is part of knowing The Writer's Advantage.

So when you do a search for this practice under "Twin Movies" or "identical movies released at the same time," you'll see that lists go back a couple decades. (Also note that this happens in publishing and with TV shows as well — see next paragraph). Some examples of this phenomenon are:

Dangerous Liaisons (1988) and *Valmont* (1989)
Jurassic Park (1993) and *Carnosaur* (1993)
Tombstone (1993) and *Wyatt Earp* (1994)
Dante's Peak (1997) and *Volcano* (1997)
Antz (1998) and *A Bug's Life* (1998)
The Truman Show (1998) and *EDtv* (1999)
Chasing Liberty (2004) and *First Daughter* (2004)
The Prestige (2006) and *The Illusionist* (2006)
Olympus Has Fallen (2013) and *White House Down* (2013)

...and so on and so forth. There are many of these twin movie examples. In most cases, one of these films performs better than the other, leaving the other one behind in cinema history without much fanfare and glory. And as I said, this happens in the publishing industry and with TV series as well.

SPOTTING TRENDS

As we look at the examples of movies and the development of similar ideas at about the same time of release, we see that this practice is fairly common and not especially desirable. Within the television industry, however, this mirroring of ideas is often what sets off a trend within a particular season. For instance, during the television seasons of 2011 through 2012, five sitcoms appeared that featured female comedic leads along with behind-the-scenes creators, producers, and crews that included a good number of women. HBO's *Girls*, CBS's *Two Broke Girls*, Fox's *New Girl*, and NBC's *Whitney* and *Are You There Chelsea?* — all produced, written by and starring young women in their twenties to thirties. Coincidence or trend?

Of these five shows, two — *Whitney* and *Are You There Chelsea?* — did not find their audiences and were cancelled. The other three tended to break ground in the world of sitcom writing in regard to the subject matter and portrayal of young women in society. The content resonated to viewers, so much so that Lena Dunham (*Girls*) has been said to be the voice of her generation, with Zooey Deschanel (*New Girl*) following close behind as the quintessential example of the "Manic Pixie Dream Girl" meme. It seems the individuals who developed these shows at the networks also had a hunch that there would be something within the seasonal arc and characters' traits that would appeal to their audiences. Each show was given an opportunity to find its audience and *New Girl*, *Two Broke Girls*, and *Girls* did just that — in fact, they found sizeable success.

These women came up at the same time as the network execs (as many folks making decisions at networks are within the late twenties to early forties age range). Whitney Cummings wrote for Chelsea Handler's talk show, so there was the factor that they were working alongside each other also, paralleling their similar energies and grabbing the opportunities to move forward. Cummings is also the creator of *Two Broke Girls*. In all cases, there was a gut feeling amongst the creators and the execs to go forward with this type of programming.

Also know that there are groups of creative individuals that complement each other and go on to create media content like this all the time. Think Tina Fey and Amy Poehler. Between the two of them, we could put together a fairly long list of projects they have touched in some way or another, whether they worked on the content directly or not. They also contributed to the reason why the women creators were able to flourish in 2011–12 as both Fey and Poehler broke ground for contemporary female writers with their many years on *Saturday Night Live* and their own sitcoms *30 Rock* (2006–2013) and *Parks and Recreation* (2009–present). You can see how they have played off one another throughout their years of creating, and the impact that has had on programming.

COPYING GENRE TRAITS

In the case of the new female-driven comedies, the shows in discussion generally held on to the basic traits seen in most sitcoms since the beginning of television time. Traits such as comedic beats including stinging one-liners, limited locations (usually a home and work set), a group of friends to add various storylines (and all of those friends have issues), and struggles of some sort for the female lead(s). These struggles revolve around work (the title *Two Broke Girls* says it all), and romance. Ultimately, as a result of going through all of the experiences they go through, the groups of friends become closer, or experience jealousy and deception, joy and fear, sexual experiences, etc. All of these traits remain in tact with this new wave of shows. So what's new?

In most cases, these shows push the limit for the females who inhabit these female-centric worlds. They go beyond where many female characters have gone in the past. One can say that *Sex and the City* (1998–2004) could be identified as the quintessential text for these sitcoms. That show led the way for these women to talk frankly about sex, drink without judgment, and make choices about their careers without male leads and male dominance. These women are completely free to do what they want to do and to talk as men have talked within sitcoms (and other TV shows and movies and books) for years. They are independent women who are exploring their lives without restraint from men, parental units, or society. The result is that we see some raw footage (especially within *Girls*) of sexual and ethical situations. They have pushed the envelope for women writers, creators, and actresses for the future. The next generation of women writers need to study their voices and understand the risks they've taken.

These women did away with compliant women characters and brought that female bravado out into the open. It worked for these shows, and this trend broke new ground for female writers for the future. There is power in taking risks, in choosing right. Studying these patterns and trends assists you and your ultimate project and brand.

TWO WAYS TO GO

When patterns and trends appear, as in this case, pay attention to them. In regard to the twin movie examples, it's a good indication that if you have a script that is similar in energy to the two that have just been produced, then it would be good for you to place that script on a shelf for awhile. The idea has been done. The audience tires of similar themes fairly quickly. It does not mean that you would not be able to sell that script at some time in the future, just not right now.

In regard to the television marketplace (and this follows for publishing also), when a trend appears on the scene, there is usually a rapid acquisition period where "knock-off" projects are sought out. This is mostly because folks who put the TV seasons together do not know anything (remember what Mr. Goldman said — "Nobody knows anything"). So they look for additional projects in the same vein for a short time after the success of the original content takes place. This is when it is up to you to decide if you want to go along with the trend or hold out and submit your new original idea.

OR, you may find a way to write an authentic version of the trending subject matter. That is, you find a way to put your own mark on the same genre. This is possible to do. It is what we have been talking about throughout this book. If you choose to do this, then take the traits of the genre and build upon them, make them your own — choose wisely what you want to include or not. You may find yourself riding on top of a creative wave and able to sell your idea on the coattails of the current trend. This usually lasts for a very small window — maybe two or three months, no more than six months, so act quickly.

If not, wait until that trend rides itself out. Then introduce your ideas. You could start the next trend.

TOOLKIT SANDBOX

Real Reality TV, Some Questions, and a Fun Lunch

CASE STUDY: WHY REALITY TV
HAS BEEN ALL THE RAGE

Here is an example of how trends happen, and it is a trend in TV that everyone knows and is perhaps a little too familiar with — Reality TV.

When producers Mark Burnett and Charlie Parsons pitched the idea of *Survivor* (2000–present) to the networks, development folks weren't entirely sure that a show about 10 to 12 individuals stranded on an island and forced to "survive" within a competition scenario would be something the American public would like to see. After all, there were only one or two reality shows on the entire TV schedule at that point, and those mostly exposed the inside world of cops and wanted men.

It wasn't until an assistant working in the development department at CBS recognized that his generation would probably find this concept to be of interest did the "big wigs" at the network take notice. That assistant's age was approximately 23 in 2000, which meant that he was 15 in 1992.

Why is this assistant's age important? Because it meant that he was probably a fan of the first few years of MTV's *The Real World* (1992–present). To him, "seven strangers living in a house..." (as the intro voice over began for every episode of one of the most favorite reality shows of all time) seemed like a great idea, as the series had enjoyed great success for many seasons at that point. He knew that his 15-year-old self enjoyed the format and that his peers did the same. And he was right. This is one scenario that clearly outlines how generations can influence trends in media. The Reality TV craze can be said to have started (the second round anyway, there was a first round in 1973 with PBS' *An American Family*, which was presented as a pure documentary), with the arrival of *Survivor* in 2000. Audiences were ready to watch a group of strangers not only live together, but compete against one another, in extreme circumstances.

There is another element that played into this successful trend and that is that in the year 2000, most Americans had been living in peaceful non-threatening decades of peacetime. A year later came the terrorist acts of September 11, and the energy of the world shifted. Light comedy seemed almost tasteless. Everyone toughened up. Competition became ordinary within normal life and being on alert was something everyone now found themselves doing — not unlike the folks on the island or in the many teenaged households of *Real World*. This trend is a combination of generational shifts and historical events shared by a group of people. There is no doubt why Reality TV, with all of its intense dog-eat-dog scrapping and fighting, has been popular for well over a decade now.

There are many different sub-genres within the Reality TV genre, and it will never completely be absent within the television landscape — however, it has peaked. This trend continues to morph and find a way to put a spin on already existing formulas. What's next for Reality TV? That's up to you to figure out. Study what an entire generation of viewers have already seen and create something above and beyond that content.

QUESTIONING WITH THE WRITER'S ADVANTAGE

1. With all of the twin movies that have appeared in the last few decades, is there one scenario where you think the lesser favorite is better than the one that is loved by most? Why?

2. When twin movies appear on the scene, do you usually see both of them to compare and contrast? Do you care that two movies are made regarding the same subject matter?

3. Are you aware of the many trends that appear in the book world, on TV, and within the film world? What is one of your favorite recent trends?

4. Do you have a favorite author or showrunner/producer you emulate? Why?

5. Have you ever thought that a favorite author or showrunner/producer jumped the shark with any of their work? Why?

6. Do you intend to follow a trend? Why?

7. Do you intend to introduce your new version of a genre? Why?

EXERCISE

MY FAVORITE WRITER

Identify your favorite author, director, or producer and make a list of all of the questions you would ask them and the topics you would like to discuss with them if you were granted a two-hour meeting. Make good choices here. Remember, the hypothetical answers would give you insight into why you are writing your material the way you are.

CHAPTER 11

CHECK-LISTING YOUR AUTHENTIC MATERIAL

You're almost there. Chapters 5 through 10 have guided you through the elements that are part of your Genre Toolkit. Your completed Genre Toolkit includes your quintessential text, the traits of the genre, an understanding of the history of the genre, along with an understanding of patterns and trends within the marketplace. You are about to move to the next level — defending your work. You are now armed with information you need to produce an authentic text. Remember that an authentic text goes beyond the original elements of a genre to produce a new and improved version of that genre. You are pretty much armed with the information you need. You got this!

CHECKING AND CHECKING AGAIN

We've arrived at the point where you'll need to cross your "t"s and dot your "i"s. Here are your checklists within the Genre Toolkit. Utilize these checklists to ensure that you have addressed all elements needed to complete your path to your authentic text. You don't want to fall short when you begin to pitch your project.

Right now. Do this now. Sit down and make these lists and check them twice for each project you are intending to take out into the marketplace.

THE WRITER'S ADVANTAGE CHECKLIST

YOUR QUINTESSENTIAL TEXT

Identify the texts that have appeared historically within your genre that best represent your genre and the type of text you're writing. List why you find these texts to be important to your material. (In most cases this should be limited to one or two texts, however there may be more — up until five — due to the type of project you may be working on.)

1. THE quintessential text (QT) is:

    And here's why:

    Here are some additional texts that are close in range to my quintessential text and why they have been necessary to study:

2. QT #2:
    Why:

3. QT #3
    Why:

4. QT #4
    Why:

5. QT #5
    Why:

TRAITS TO MAINTAIN

What traits are inherent to your genre and what has been working throughout most of the successful texts in said genre?

List 10 to 15 common traits:

1.

2.

3.

4.

5.

6.

7.

8.

9.

10.

11.

12.

13.

14.

15.

TRAITS TO DELETE

What traits have fallen away within the genre due to shifts in audience popularity, generational shifts, and traits that have played themselves out?

List 10 to 15 deleted traits:

1.

2.

3.

4.

5.

6.

7.

8.

9.

10.

11.

12.

13.

14.

15.

TRAITS UNIQUE TO YOUR TEXT

What traits have you identified that are lacking in the existing way that the genre has repeatedly and/or recently been depicted? What is your version of an authentic text in this genre going to add or delete that will produce your authentic text within this genre?

List 5 to 10 unique traits:

1.

2.

3.

4.

5.

6.

7.

8.

9.

10.

NOTES ON INFORMATION FOUND
REGARDING THE TRAITS IN YOUR GENRE:

Use this space to make a note of any thoughts about the traits of your genre.

IDENTIFY THE MASS PRODUCTION
HISTORY OF YOUR GENRE:

Has your genre found an audience decade after decade, generation after generation?

Make a list of popular texts within your genre. These texts should scream out "romantic comedy" or "buddy movie" or "psychological horror," etc., meaning you should begin to see a pattern among this list of texts within your genre that have proved themselves over the years.

List 5 to 10 popular texts:

1.
2.
3.
4.
5.
6.
7.
8.
9.
10.

NOTES ON INFORMATION FOUND REGARDING THE HISTORY OF YOUR GENRE:

Use this space to make a note of any thoughts about the history of your genre.

HAVE THE TEXTS WITHIN YOUR GENRE EXPERIENCED MASS ACCEPTANCE OR CULT HONOR?

This is another way of identifying why certain texts succeed or fail within their marketplaces.

List 5 to 10 wildly popular texts and then list 5 to 10 cult texts within your genre:

POPULAR

1.
2.
3.
4.
5.

6.

7.

8.

9.

10.

    CULT

1.

2.

3.

4.

5.

6.

7.

8.

9.

10.

NOTES ON INFORMATION FOUND REGARDING THE MASS OR CULT ACCEPTANCE OF YOUR GENRE:

Use this space to make a note of any thoughts about the mass or cult acceptance of your genre.

IDENTIFY THE PATTERNS OF YOUR GENRE

Have there been similar movies, series, books, web series produced around the same time regarding your genre? List why you think this may have happened.

List similar texts and why — at lease 5 examples:

1. Similar texts —
   Why:

2. Similar texts —
   Why:

3. Similar texts —
    Why:

4. Similar texts —
    Why:

5. Similar texts —
    Why:

IDENTIFY THE TRENDS OF YOUR GENRE

Has there been a recent (within the last 3 to 5 years) trend that has occurred within your genre?

Name the trend, give examples of the texts that fulfilled the trend and why. At least 5 examples.

1. Trend —
    Texts:

    Why:

2. Trend —
    Texts:

    Why:

3. Trend —
    Texts:

    Why:

4. Trend —
    Texts:

    Why:

5. Trend —
    Texts:

    Why:

NOTES ON INFORMATION FOUND REGARDING THE PATTERNS OR TRENDS OF YOUR GENRE:

Use this space to make a note of any thoughts about the patterns or trends of your genre.

YOUR CHECKLIST IS NOW COMPLETED

Now is the time to gather the information and process the next step. That step is the path that you'll take in either writing your authentic text, revising your authentic text, and/or pitching your authentic text.

You'll see that the information you have researched that appears within these lists will benefit you when it is time to defend your work. We will examine that step in the next chapter.

WHAT WOULD AN AUTHENTIC VERSION OF YOUR TEXT LOOK LIKE WITHIN YOUR GENRE? (THE ANSWER IS YOUR WORK)

You've now completed your research of your genre and by doing so, you've identified the specifics of your idea. You should be at a point where you are able to discuss your genre from an authentic writer's advantage.

The combination of your fanaticism for the genre and an enthusiasm to bring to the table new, fresh elements to present a better version of said genre will result in your achieving positive response to your idea.

Additionally, due to the above research you've conducted, you're now aware of what has been done in the past and those elements you wish to avoid and those you wish to retain, along with new elements you wish to introduce into the mix that are unique to your version of the genre.

DON'T HESITATE, OWN THIS INFORMATION WITH CONFIDENCE

If you are having difficulty with this aspect of prepping your work, that's normal. Many writers utilize this information during their conceptualization, development, and writing/re-writing of their material — and that's all fine — however, now that you'll be looking at moving your work out into the world, there's a natural tendency toward wanting to be shy. No need for shyness. Own this work you've done, be confident. You'll find that you are heavily armed with information about your project at this point. This knowledge will separate you from your competition. It will also help you understand where you will fit into the marketplace.

SECTION THREE

GETTING YOUR WORK OUT INTO THE WORLD

CHAPTER 12

DEFENDING YOUR WORK

You've completed your research. You have the insider's advantage, and after applying what you've learned about your genre, your material is ready to be pitched. Now is when you'll need to think like a potential buyer.

As mentioned earlier in this book, there are individuals who read and evaluate projects for publishers, production companies, studios, networks and web sites, who develop content in their respective fields. When you see your project from their point of view you'll begin to understand fully how to defend your work. So what's the best way to go about getting to the insider's view of these threshold guardians and what they might be looking for? Here are some questions you may encounter while you go through your journey to move your project out into the world, along with some resources to assist you. Remember that if you are self-publishing your manuscript (fiction or nonfiction) or producing your film/TV series/web series independently, it is also imperative that you have these questions answered. Somewhere along your path you'll need to obtain financial assistance and/or distribution for your material. Many of these questions and scenarios will apply and you'll need to defend yourself within that DIY scenario as well.

SOME BASIC QUESTIONS TO PONDER

In Chapter 4 I explained the basic questions every development exec asks when evaluating material, and those questions are worth repeating again. They are:

1. Why make this project?
2. Why make this project now?
3. Who cares?

The research you have gathered from Chapters 6 through 10 provide you with the basic answers you'll need to defend these questions. For instance, with the "Why make this project?" question, go to the lists of previous texts that have experienced success (and cult) status in your genre. It has been proven that everyone loves a good mystery novel, a horror film, or romance novel... by that I mean, these genres are not going anywhere. There is a base audience for your project. You'll use the lists of films, books, TV series, and web series that you've gathered to prove that your genre is solid. And while it is not the best move to begin your pitch or query with "my movie is this movie meets that movie" or "my book is this book meets that book," you might find that sometime during your pitch/query you'll mention some aspect from another well-known text in your genre in an organic manner.

Most execs are over the "this meets that" type of pitch, so definitely never begin your pitch/query in this manner. This is information to have in the back of your head to back you up — and to show that you know your genre.

As far as the next basic question "Why make this project now?" — you are also prepared to answer that, as you have completed running the history on your genre. Here is where you'll bring to the forefront your knowledge of the trends and patterns within your genre. You can also gauge generational and cultural changes in the recent past to defend why your idea would work in the future. And this is where you introduce your new version — the new traits, the spin, the reason why your authentic version will be ideal for this particular production company, publisher, network, etc., to produce now. And so, there you are, telling the potential buyer why your idea is perfect for the spirit of the times and that it needs to be made — now.

And finally, the question "Who cares?" As mentioned in Chapter 4, you'll need to know your audience. You've written a new vampire novel — who will care? Everyone (or a good percentage of those) who read *Twilight*. And why? Because your spin, your authentic version, captures the imagination of a particular group of readers (notice I didn't say "will capture" —always pitch as if the audience has already embraced your idea), and then jump into your new traits and the new version that will attract that *Twilight* base along with others in your targeted audience. Make sure you have an answer for this one and remember that just because there may be a group of individuals who study your subject matter, you must be able to provide percentages and statistics showing that that same group also BUYS books, ATTENDS movies, WATCHES television series, etc. And I know you are passionate about your projects, however the bottom line is what happens business-wise. Look to financial reports — box office reports, ratings, and bestseller lists — for this info.

BECOME YOUR OWN PRIVATE DEVELOPMENT DEPARTMENT

I mentioned previously (in Chapter 10) that you may need to ask yourself if you are intending to introduce or follow a new trend. In order to intelligently address that question, you'll need to know the landscape of the market you are about to navigate. So, how do you do that?

You do that by becoming your own private development department.

In the past, while folks developed ideas for the original studios and networks discussed in Chapter 1, they didn't have access to any information about what the other competing entities were developing. In fact, projects in development were kept in complete secrecy and no one knew about them until they began to be promoted for the upcoming "New Fall Season" and/or Holiday or Summer Box Office schedule. Gradually, through some sneak previews for movies and pilot and premiere episodes for TV series, the public started to know what the new content was, but up until that point, everyone was in the dark.

Not so today. Today you have no excuse as a great deal of this information is available via industry dedicated websites and accompanying e-newsletters. And most of these resources are free or available at a reasonable fee, you only need to sign-up or subscribe.

For information about book projects — recently signed and published digitally or traditionally:

nathanbransford.com
janefriedman.com
the-millions.com
publisherslunch.com
writersdigest.com
goodreads.com
therumpus.net
thenervousbreakdown.com
pw.org
pred-ed.com

digitalbookworld.com
thebookseller.com
kirkusreviews.com
bookexpoamerica.com

For information about feature film projects signed and in development:

deadlinehollywood.com
hollywoodreporter.com
variety.com
hollywoodwiretap.com
wifv.org
imdb.com
donedealpro.com
inktip.com
scriptcity.com
boxofficemojo.com
the-numbers.com

For information about projects signed and in development for TV:

deadlinehollywood.com
programminginsider.com (go to *adweek.com* and click on newsletters to subscribe)
cynopsis.com
cynopsis.com – digital
cynopsis.com — kids

For information about projects for web-based content:

cynopsis.com — digital

Access this information daily. Follow your specific media and genre. Make a note of not only the buyers and producers, but the agents and managers who have negotiated the deals.

You'll track your similar projects during the next few months, possibly years, to see if they actually get made or not. You will also use this information within your pitches as you defend your work as many (if not all) of the potential buyers you'll be pitching to and querying are also following these web-based resources AND also know about projects they are involved with that are not made public. So you may come up against a question within a pitch that asks "Are you aware that Grand Central Publishing just made a deal with such-and-such author for her second literary fiction novel?" and you would be able to say yes. You'll impress the potential buyer with your knowledge of insider industry news. This is also your opportunity to jump in and state WHY your idea is better than or more appropriate for that publisher to purchase.

Arm yourself with as much information possible to defend your work. Know your competition and know how you will answer questions about that content. Having this awareness places you in the best light with potential buyers. This also ensures that you are not one of the clueless types who decides to write a particular piece of content and stays sheltered in their parents' basement or their own attic away from their kids and refuses to gain knowledge about what the marketplace is yielding. They go to pitch and are shocked when potential buyers look at them and laugh. No idea on its own is great enough to sell without knowing the marketplace you are selling it within.

SOME DEEPER QUESTIONS TO PONDER

Continuing to navigate the marketplace as your own personal development department assists you when you are asked questions such as the following:

TIMELINESS ELEMENTS —

1. How will your project resonate to audiences a year to 18 months from now?

2. How will your project continue to resonate to audiences 5 years out? (In other words, is your project "evergreen" material that the company will reap the benefits from year after year. Another way to answer this is to see your project listed as a quintessential text or, at the very least, within the list of top ten in its genre.)

3. How does your project fit into the current landscape (with current trends) and do you see it becoming a trend if it is not following along with other trends?

GENERATIONAL/SOCIETY ELEMENTS —

1. Will all generations and attention spans want to read/watch your content? If not, why? (Defend this by explaining that you are seeking out only a specific part of the audience, which may be appropriate for some projects).

2. Is there a current trend in society or with a specific generation that supports your idea? Provide evidence of this trend with accompanying print/web articles and social media forums.

3. Is there something about your content that might offend a part of society or a specific generation?

    Additionally, there may be casting questions (for film, TV, and web-based projects) and budgeting questions for material that features exotic locales, period piece scenarios, or spans decades of time. At this point, don't worry too much about those specific questions, as it is the story that is important. Content is king; all other budgeting issues and casting elements can be negotiated and resolved once the project is purchased.

EXERCISE

TESTING YOUR IDEA UNTIL IT IS FOOLPROOF

To test your idea, run it through the Basic Cable menu within your local cable provider's list. (Even if you don't have cable, you can access Time Warner, Comcast, Charter's Basic Cable menu through their websites.) Take your idea and imagine how it would play and be promoted on NBC, then how it would look if it were produced by BRAVO, or ESPN, or LOGO, etc. This seems like it might be a lot of unnecessary work, but it isn't and here's why. By doing this exercise you'll be taken out of your comfort zone. For the entire duration of this method so far you have been working with honing and defining material within a specific genre. Now I'm asking you to explore your idea beyond the way you see it within its format and push the limits of the idea. Oftentimes you'll find areas within your storyline/general theme/plot that need to be developed that you didn't even think of or were aware of. No need to spend hours doing this, just a quick look. Jot down any thoughts that come to mind as you do this. You'll be surprised —pleasantly surprised.

If you are averse to cable networks, then go to Amazon or a Netflix menu and run your idea through all of the different genres. Imagine what your vampire novel might look like as a western, as a creative nonfiction entry, or as a sports book, etc.

Navigate the marketplace, record information about your genre and similar projects, continue to track and comb the necessary resources, and you will be ready to defend your work.

Use The Writer's Advantage to the best of your ability. Arm yourself. Be prepared. Onward!

CHAPTER 13

WHAT MASTERING YOUR GENRE CAN DO FOR YOU

Mastering your genre is power. At the beginning of this book I discussed how audiences have short attention spans, are fragmented, and that there are generational differences throughout the transmedia marketplace. The result has been, in recent years, a somewhat broken, discombobulated, and disconnected collective consciousness.

LIKE-MINDED AWARENESS

Writing with The Writer's Advantage and utilizing the Genre Toolkit List elevates your awareness of your project(s) and how you present yourself within this arena. Your pitch and selling materials, including your loglines and synopses, will be based on research and facts, and enhanced with your enthusiasm. Gone are weak scripts and manuscripts that are based on one-dimensional ideas. Additionally, clueless "Stormy Weather" deliveries and pitches of said material are also gone. Instead of remakes, reboots, sequels and prequels, original authentic material permeates the marketplace once again and writers, development execs, producers and agents alike recognize the new idea enlightenment. Presenting authentic material will attract like-minded people who are looking for those authentic ideas.

Along with the raising up of a whole new collective consciousness filled with authentic ideas, your content resonates accordingly. This happens whether you honor your existing genre as it is or bring something new to the table by presenting a game-changer element, a spin on the genre, or offer up an exciting new sub-genre. You've mastered your genre, now it's time to move your good work out into the world.

You are also aware of how your content will appear within this marketplace knowing that you may be writing a novel that will eventually appear as a TV series or feature film, or you may be writing a reality TV franchise that could easily be edited into webseries segments. Understanding how your content will spread across all platforms gives you an advantage for potential sales in all transmedia platforms.

As you prepare your material to be shopped within this marketplace, continue to access the e-newsletters and websites suggested in Chapter 12. I have mentioned throughout this book about those writers who work with blinders on or in their attics and basements without any awareness of the world around them. When they emerge to present their work they are shocked that someone else has just sold a project that mirrors their own. If they had been monitoring these sources, they would have known about this material being picked up and could have 1.) altered their project so it would not be competition to the other piece, or 2.) put the project on hold for a while until it feels fresh again.

ALTERING

A couple of years ago a student of mine wrote an epic tale of a young girl who sets out on her path to destiny within a dystopian society, only to learn that she must fight her way to the top of her kingdom in order to obtain the wisdom of her elders who were, in fact, a race of superior Amazon-like women. The manuscript's first five to six chapters were similar to *The Hunger Games* — an almost identical plot. The writer's work was superb, well researched, brilliant. He had been crafting this epic tale for nearly a decade and was ready to go out with it right after *The Hunger Games* appeared on the scene. We had to discuss his selling strategy because editors would clearly see this resemblance and either disregard the work or consider it — if good enough — to be a project that could be sold in the shadow of the now-iconic *Hunger Games*. The writer continued to receive rejections. His manuscript was just too close in execution to *Hunger Games*. What to do next? He decided that he worked too hard and too long on the project to just give it up, so he went the self-publishing route. Armed with determination and knowledge of the marketplace, he earned a small following by starting out with a group of young readers at his local library. Those readers and the local librarians told other readers and other librarians (librarians can be very influential) and the book found its readership.

PUT IT ON HOLD

Another student of mine had written a solid animation script about talking cars. The writer worked on this script for nearly a year, researched the market very well and determined that cars had never been awarded personalities and voices in an animated fashion. He was just about ready to shop it when I read that Disney and Pixar were developing a project about, well, just that — animated cars with personalities and voices — the movie *Cars* (2006). The writer had to put that script away and move on to the next one, which was the best move he could make. He would have looked like an idiot going in and pitching an animated movie about cars after this project was announced.

TOOLS YOU'LL NEED TO SELL YOUR AUTHENTIC TEXT(S)

Many in the industry consider the buying-selling pitching scenario to be a big game and in a way, it is. Essentially, if you think of it in that way, you'll be more relaxed when you do begin to email, call, and pitch your project to industry buyers. In order to continue to prepare yourself, you'll need two essential items in addition to all of the great research and background information you already have about your genre. You need to compose a logline and a synopsis.

LOGLINE

Your logline must be in place before you begin to talk to anyone about your project. Think of your logline as a way to explain your project without giving away too much information. It is an important item because you want to intrigue and entice the potential buyer with it. The logline should be one or two solid sentences in length.

Begin with your main character (if you have a piece that features an ensemble, begin with them; e.g., a group of friends at a reunion), then add the basic scenario that character(s) find themselves in and introduce the pending conflict or doom they'll need to resolve.

Character + scenario + conflict needed to be resolved.

Examples:

Peter's Ponzi Predicament
Peter Mathers doesn't want to be a Starbucks barista for the rest of his life and becomes involved with a group who promise him he'll make money fast. Things are going well until he

realizes it might be too late to get out of being dead center in one of the world's largest Ponzi schemes.

Within this example, a dramatic premise is presented. Included in this idea are two scenarios that are prominent within the current time frame of the project being pitched. Including these types of scenarios answers that "why make this now?" question.

A young man is tired of working a mediocre job (Starbucks barista) and seeks out another way to make money, falling into a potentially bad financial scheming process. Ponzi schemes have been in the news, and in a world that is economically striving, they aren't going to go away very soon. You would defend this logline with other texts that include young people taking risks to better themselves (a typical scenario) such as *21* (2008), *Oceans 11, 12, 13* (2001, 2004, 2007), *Rounders* (1998), and so on. This pitch includes the research you've been conducting throughout the book. You'll be prepared to state why your idea is better than the others and why your idea is necessary in today's marketplace due to the relevance of the subject matter. This research gives you The Writer's Advantage.

Another example:

You can also incorporate your genre knowledge composing something like this:

Lire's Library
In the spirit of famous libraries, little Annie Lire stumbles upon a secret library that holds the interactive manuscripts of the sequels to all of the world's great children's books. Annie, with the help of the world's famous literary characters, wants to ensure that the sequels are made available to all children, but a powerful publishing conglomerate has a different idea.

This idea is exploding with excellent tropes of pop culture from a number of different points. Think of all of the famous libraries in literature — Hogwarts Library, the library used in *The Breakfast Club*, The Jedi Archives, the Beast's library in *Beauty and the Beast*, the libraries in *Ever After*, and *Clue,* and so on. Take those great visual scenes and combine them with children's classics such as *Mother Goose* and *Winnie the Pooh* and *Alice In Wonderland* and you have an idea that explodes off the page. As your main character navigates her newly found world of the interactive characters (think what *Shrek* did when referencing Disney characters) and add the urgency of an evil corporation and you have a winning idea. This idea could easily shine as a new classic children's franchise — perhaps one to replace Harry Potter? It is truly evergreen. All development departments and editors/publishers are on that search — why not be the one to fill that void?

Be ready to use the research you've completed within your Genre Toolkit when you defend your work within your query letters/emails and all pitches in general.

SYNOPSIS

A synopsis is a one-page summary of your project. Think about all of those book reports you wrote in grade school. Essentially, you are telling the potential buyer what your manuscript, script, webseries is about via a one page, single-spaced document.

Many writers find it difficult to reduce their complex storylines into one page. Nonetheless, you'll need to do this. This is a document that will precede your completed manuscript or script. The potential buyer must be able to comprehend your storyline and see the overall scope of your project within this one page document. It leads, hopefully, to their wanting to see the entire manuscript or script.

The secret to writing an effective synopsis is simple. Write three paragraphs:

— the first paragraph is your first act or set-up of your story.

— the second paragraph is your second act; the conflict.

— the third paragraph is your plot's movement towards resolution.

Tell your story fast and sure. Establish the basics and get through your plot points. It is that simple. Over and done.

GOING OUT

Armed with these tools that represent your work, it is now time to begin to shop your project. The first item of business is to register your work with *copyright.gov* (if you have a completed manuscript) and/or the Writers Guild of America at *wga.org* for ideas and completed scripts. The fees are minimal and you will receive a registered number that proves that your work is yours should there ever be a question about plagiarism of your work in the future.

With a manuscript or book proposal you can query agents who work within the genres you represent and you can query publishers directly.

With a script, you can query agents and production companies and producers directly.

No matter what media you are working within, you should send out as many queries as possible at one time to as many places that you feel represent similar subject matter.

You'll do some more research here. There are excellent resources for literary agents such as *imdbpro.com* for production companies and producers and the *Writer's Digest* List of Literary Agents for manuscript submissions. In today's world, most legitimate agents and production companies have websites that instruct you as to how to submit your query information. *Follow those instructions exactly.* Do not deliberately leave out an item they request or submit a manuscript when they ask for only a logline and synopsis. This is a long process, practically a full-time job, actually. Most folks who take on the process of shopping their project set aside one or two hours a day to send their queries and continue along that path until they sell their work.

Keep a clear and concise paper trail of where and to whom you are sending your work.

You'll need this in case you find that someone has ripped off your work later on in the game. Record the company, the person you are sending your work to, their assistant, and date/time. Also have a column for the result of that query. Maintain this list throughout your shopping process.

The next steps are to embrace the rejections (every rejection leads onward to the next door that may open with a resounding "yes"). Study the rejections — you can learn a great deal about your work through the information received via rejections. Yes, they are not what you are expecting, but it doesn't mean your project is bad or wrong, it just means you haven't found the right place for it to grow. This process is as complicated as finding the right job or right romantic partner... and yes, you have to kiss a lot of frogs, so to speak, in order to get to your princely publisher or production company.

PITCH FESTS AND CONFERENCES

In addition to cold calling/emailing your work, you can also attend any of the many annual pitch fests and conferences that are scheduled year round. These are excellent arenas to meet with agents and potential buyers via a 3- to 8- to 10-minute meeting where you pitch your logline and then go into your storyline (synopsis info). If the potential buyer is intrigued with your idea, they will ask to see more.

These events are held for both literary writers and screenwriters.

Literary events can be accessed through *Writer's Digest* at *writersdigest.com*.

Screenwriting events can be accessed through The Writer's Store at *writersstore.com*.

In many cases, you can pitch manuscripts at screenwriting events also.

MASTERING YOUR GENRE

Congratulations, you mastered your genre! You've completed the research and have your selling materials in hand. You are light years ahead of most writers marketing and pitching their work for the first — or fortieth — time. The research you've uncovered arms you so you'll be able to answer most questions about your genre and your project's place in the transmedia marketplace. You've proceeded to move ahead of the others. You now have The Writer's Advantage.

EXERCISE

WRITE YOUR LOGLINE AND SYNOPSIS

Based on your research, construct a logline and synopsis that attracts the potential buyer into wanting to see more — and eventually publishing and/or producing your work. (If you want to stretch your wings, write your own synopsis for *Lire's Library.*)

CHAPTER 14

WHAT ELSE HAVE YOU GOT?

I spent about a year and a half writing my first novel. It was the usual "here's the story of my first major romantic love-affair-post-break-up" novel set in Los Angeles in the 1980s. After many queries I had garnered the attention of a major book agent in L.A. We had a meeting at his office in West Hollywood. I was ecstatic, to say the least, feeling nervous and awkward as every first-time novelist does. We had a long conversation about the book, about how he was going to send it to some New York folks for their perusal and then his agency, along with a New York based agency, would figure out what publishing houses to present it to.

Heady stuff. At the end of the meeting he asked me, "So, what else have you got?" I gasped a bit, and answered with total honesty. "Nothing. I've spent the last two years of my life on that manuscript you have in your hands. I haven't had time to write anything else," to which he responded with the absolute best piece of advice I have ever received in my career overall.

"My dear, never answer that question again in that way, ever."

Little did I know that I had already lost the publication deal at that point. There were a number of other hoops and barrels that I had to jump through during the evaluation process of that first project, and in the end it never found a publishing house. I know in retrospect that I lost a great deal of credibility when I answered that golden question with "Nothing."

By answering "Nothing" it meant that I was not an established writer, and that is sometimes all right if your first effort is something of a rarity that blasts on the scene for whatever reason, resonates to an audience, and locks into a successful sales run. However, in most cases, these agents are looking to represent a writer who has a body of work that will prove to be a cash cow. The selling of one first novel was going to garner him enough money to pay for a nice lunch, not the amount he would have made if I would have had at least one more manuscript in the hopper and two or three more ideas ready to be written. Instead, he had a maybe-writer who would see if her novel would sell and then maybe-possibly write another one and that added up to only maybe-possible money.

I was writing as a hobby — or at least it looked that way. I wasn't a serious writer. I wasn't a player. Basically, I wasn't bankable.

PLAYERS VS. PIKERS

The responses you give to questions asked during your exchanges to sell your material will be the difference between your career as a writer who is to be taken seriously — a player in the industry, or your being seen as what we call a piker. A piker is someone who is just pretending to climb up the mountain and isn't really planning to, or going to, actually reach the peak.

This search for materials to be published and produced is not a hobby to these skilled professionals. They are listening to your pitch, evaluating your query letters, and weighing the profitability of your manuscripts and scripts with precise expertise and sincere intentions. It is for this main reason that you will need to have at least three to five additional projects ready to be pitched. That is, have at least one other project near-to-completion and have loglines and synopses for at least four to five projects. Now, you may not have any materials to back these up and be in the same situation that I was, having devoted all of your precious available time outside your job and personal life to writing your first manuscript, but you must still present yourself as someone who has a body of work.

Additionally, by flexing your muscles and composing other selling materials for future projects, you begin to see your brand. You begin to see where you might want to go with your work in the future. As you completed the exercises of Chapters 5 through 12, you gathered some other thoughts about potential additional manuscripts and scripts. These will be your answer to "What else have you got?"

DON'T BE A TEASE

Do not query agents, publishers, production companies and/or producers unless you have entire manuscripts and scripts to show them. This is a hard and fast rule. There are always those writers who fall into the "wanna be" category. I say "wanna be" because they will never move past that level of being unknown to being published or produced if they do not have completed projects to present after they've pitched them.

Wanna-be writers make the statement "I'm going to pitch this idea and if they like it or buy it, then I'll write it." I've seen this happen over and over. A writer will attend a pitch fest, pitch their idea, and the potential buyer asks for the manuscript or script. The writer emails or texts me in a "high importance/

frantic" mode asking what to do. I respond with "Write the script. Now. Immediately. Don't go to sleep until it is finished. If you do not send that material to them within a 24 to 48 hour period, they will forget about the idea, and worse, know that you are an amateur, a piker, a wanna-be."

AUTHENTIC WRITING

As a writer who has now been introduced to The Writer's Advantage and to the necessary tools you need to use to create material that will represent your genre in a new and improved way, here are three standards to follow:

Do not pitch your projects until you have completed the Genre Toolkit List research found in this book.

Do not pitch your projects until they are completed and ready to be seen in a professional marketplace.

Do not pitch your projects unless you have additional follow-up material to present as part of your work as a writer.

You want to be taken seriously — and you will when you present yourself as a vibrant creator of content that offers something new to these potential buyers.

WHAT NOW?

You've organized your research for one project and you can use that same method over and over again for your next projects. If you work within the same genre, then you'll be building upon the research you completed for your first project. Mastering one genre can also help as you master another.

NO FEAR OF SUCCESS

Know what you want as you go out into the world with your material. Know what you want to ask for. In other words, do you want to sell your material straight away and receive a lump sum payment, or are you thinking that you would like to be involved as a creative producer should, say, your manuscript be picked up as a TV series with the WB or on Netflix. You can ask for whatever you envision.

Know this. Too often writers are a timid type who do not think that they deserve the success of selling their work or posting their work digitally and finding a following. You'll never know until you do this (note that I didn't say "try this," because in this world, as in Yoda's world, there are no "tries," only do or do not). You've racked up a number of hours performing this research, writing your manuscript or script, and prepping your selling materials. Don't stop there.

Too many writers have a fear of success. Yes, I said success. Why? Because they know that when they sell their material their life is going to change. And it is going to change, and you'll have control over that also when you reach that level.

For now, believe that you will sell your work, if that is what you want to do, and know that it is not a matter of "if" but "when" you find a way to distribute your work to those audiences who will benefit from your work.

You are now an authentic writer. You've crafted a project that reflects your own voice, your vision. You have something new to offer to the marketplace with valid, solid facts to back up your project. Your confidence level is high because you know where your material fits into the marketplace. This information will assist you throughout your writing career.

This method works. It shares the insider knowledge found in development departments and editors' offices with you, the writer, so you won't look like an idiot when you go out with your work. You also won't be pitching an idea that's been heard and done a million times over — you'll be pitching a new, authentic text.

You have not only mastered your genre, you've mastered The Writer's Advantage.

EXERCISE

KEEP WRITING

Write loglines and synopses for at least three to five of your additional projects and keep writing forward....

A FEW LAST WORDS

I have worked with many writers who have been successful in their own right in the entertainment and publishing industries. The most joyous texts, emails, and calls I receive are those from writers I've worked with who have achieved their goals. Their goals vary. One could be that of completing their manuscript/script, and another could be that of selling their work as a three-book franchise or feature deal. Progress to me means any step along the way, from completion to sale, and I happily applaud their achievements. If they followed my advice and incorporated some element we discussed into their work, I am thankful and consider the news to be a tiny bit of a success on my behalf also.

I have always felt that this is information that is my duty to share, information that was passed down to me from my mentors and colleagues, along with my learned experience throughout my two career paths.

There is a saying in the entertainment industry: "You're only as good as your last movie, or book, etc." In my case, I'm only as good as my last successful student(s).

Long ago I wished that I could be available to assist as many writers as the number of shells that appeared on the beach I had been visiting in Ventura, California.

I have met many, many of those lovely shells and have been fortunate to work with them and I look forward to meeting the others, thanking them along the way for seeking me out at the right time and right place and for taking the time to learn The Writer's Advantage.

ABOUT THE AUTHOR

Photo by Laura Kahl

Laurie Scheer, Media Goddess, is a former vice president of programming for WE: Women's Entertainment. She has worked as an assistant, d-girl, and producer for ABC, Viacom, Showtime, and AMC-Cablevision. She has also been involved in producing digital-based forms of entertainment.

Laurie has been an instructor at numerous universities across the U.S., from UCLA to Yale. She is the author of a book about working in Hollywood entitled *Creative Careers in Hollywood* and her DVD *How to Pitch and Sell Your Screenplay* has been a perennial favorite at screenwriting events. As a professional speaker, she has appeared at annual industry conferences. She has served as a judge for numerous screenplay competitions, film festivals, and the International Emmys.

She is part of the faculty at UW-Madison's Continuing Studies Writing Department and the Director of their annual Writer's Institute. In 2013 she became the Managing Editor of *Midwest Prairie Review*. As recognition for mentoring and upholding the social responsibility of media professionals, she is the recipient of the 2014 James T. Tiedge

Memorial Award through her undergraduate alma mater, Marquette University.

The Writer's Advantage: A Toolkit for Mastering Your Genre continues her commitment to exploring ways to preserve good storytelling within the 21st century transmedia marketplace.

THE WRITER'S JOURNEY
3RD EDITION

MYTHIC STRUCTURE FOR WRITERS

CHRISTOPHER VOGLER

BEST SELLER
OVER 170,000 COPIES SOLD!

See why this book has become an international best seller and a true classic. *The Writer's Journey* explores the powerful relationship between mythology and storytelling in a clear, concise style that's made it required reading for movie executives, screenwriters, playwrights, scholars, and fans of pop culture all over the world.

Both fiction and nonfiction writers will discover a set of useful myth-inspired storytelling paradigms (i.e., "The Hero's Journey") and step-by-step guidelines to plot and character development. Based on the work of Joseph Campbell, *The Writer's Journey* is a must for all writers interested in further developing their craft.

The updated and revised third edition provides new insights and observations from Vogler's ongoing work on mythology's influence on stories, movies, and man himself.

"This book is like having the smartest person in the story meeting come home with you and whisper what to do in your ear as you write a screenplay. Insight for insight, step for step, Chris Vogler takes us through the process of connecting theme to story and making a script come alive."
> – Lynda Obst, Producer, *Sleepless in Seattle, How to Lose a Guy in 10 Days;* Author, *Hello, He Lied*

"This is a book about the stories we write, and perhaps more importantly, the stories we live. It is the most influential work I have yet encountered on the art, nature, and the very purpose of storytelling."
> – Bruce Joel Rubin, Screenwriter, *Stuart Little 2, Deep Impact, Ghost, Jacob's Ladder*

CHRISTOPHER VOGLER is a veteran story consultant for major Hollywood film companies and a respected teacher of filmmakers and writers around the globe. He has influenced the stories of movies from *The Lion King* to *Fight Club* to *The Thin Red Line* and most recently wrote the first installment of *Ravenskull*, a Japanese-style manga or graphic novel. He is the executive producer of the feature film *P.S. Your Cat is Dead* and writer of the animated feature *Jester Till*.

$26.95 · 300 PAGES · ORDER NUMBER 76RLS · ISBN: 193290736x

THE SCRIPT-SELLING GAME
A HOLLYWOOD INSIDER'S LOOK AT GETTING YOUR
SCRIPT SOLD AND PRODUCED

KATHIE FONG YONEDA

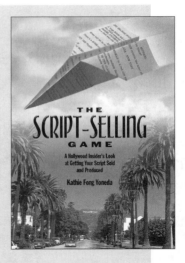

There are really only two types of people in Hollywood: those who sit around wearing black clothes in smoky coffee shops, complaining they can't get their scripts past the studio gates... and then there are the players. The ones with the hot scripts. The ones crackling with energy. The ones with knowledge.

Players understand that their success in Hollywood is not based on luck or nepotism; it's the result of understanding how Hollywood really works.

The Script-Selling Game brings together over 25 years of experience from an entertainment professional who shows you how to prepare your script, pitch it, meet the moguls, talk the talk, and make the deal. It's a must for both novice and veteran screenwriters.

"Super-concise, systematic, real-world advice on the practical aspects of screenwriting and mastering Hollywood from a professional. This book will save you time, embarrassment, and frustration and will give you an extra edge in taking on the studio system."
> — Christopher Vogler, Author, *The Writer's Journey: Mythic Structure for Writers*, Seminar Leader, former Story Consultant with Fox 2000

"I've been extremely fortunate to have Kathie's insightful advice and constructive criticism on my screenplays. She has been a valued mentor to me. Now, through this wonderful book, she can be your mentor, as well."
> — Pamela Wallace, Academy Award® Co-Winner, Best Writing, Screenplay Written Directly for the Screen, *Witness*

"This book is essential, invaluable, and necessary for any screenwriter wanting to make it in the competitive buyer's world. Yoneda gives the screenwriter the insider's view in a kind, encouraging, insightful way, and makes the impossible seem possible."
> — Dr. Linda S. Seger, Script Consultant and Author, *And the Best Screenplay Goes to...* , *Making A Good Script Great*, *Creating Unforgettable Characters*, *Making A Good Writer Great*

KATHIE FONG YONEDA is an industry veteran, currently under contract to Paramount TV in their Longform Division, and an independent script consultant whose clientele includes several award-winning writers. Kathie also conducts workshops based on *The Script-Selling Game* in the U.S. and Europe.

$16.95 · 196 PAGES · ORDER NUMBER 100RLS · ISBN: 0941188442

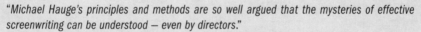

SAVE THE CAT! GOES TO THE MOVIES
THE SCREENWRITER'S GUIDE TO EVERY STORY EVER TOLD

BLAKE SNYDER

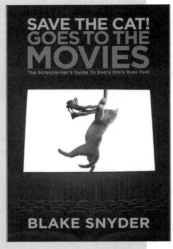

In the long-awaited sequel to his surprise bestseller, *Save the Cat!*, author and screenwriter Blake Snyder returns to form in a fast-paced follow-up that proves why his is the most talked-about approach to screenwriting in years. In the perfect companion piece to his first book, Snyder delivers even more insider's information gleaned from a 20-year track record as "one of Hollywood's most successful spec screenwriters," giving you the clues to write *your* movie.

Designed for screenwriters, novelists, and movie fans, this book gives readers the key breakdowns of the 50 most instructional movies from the past 30 years. From *M*A*S*H* to *Crash*, from *Alien* to *Saw*, from *10* to *Eternal Sunshine of the Spotless Mind*, Snyder reveals how screenwriters who came before you tackled the same challenges you are facing with the film you want to write — or the one you are currently working on.

Writing a "rom-com"? Check out the "Buddy Love" chapter for a "beat for beat" dissection of *When Harry Met Sally...* plus references to 10 other great romantic comedies that will make your story sing.

Want to execute a great mystery? Go to the "Whydunit" section and learn about the "dark turn" that's essential to the heroes of *All the President's Men*, *Blade Runner*, *Fargo* and hip noir *Brick* — and see why ALL good stories, whether a Hollywood blockbuster or a Sundance award winner, follow the same rules of structure outlined in Snyder's breakthrough method.

If you want to sell your script and create a movie that pleases most audiences most of the time, the odds increase if you reference Snyder's checklists and see what makes 50 films tick. After all, both executives and audiences respond to the same elements good writers seek to master. They want to know the type of story they signed on for, and whether it's structured in a way that satisfies everyone. It's what they're looking for. And now, it's what you can deliver.

BLAKE SNYDER, besides selling million-dollar scripts to both Disney and Spielberg, is still "one of Hollywood's most successful spec screenwriters," having made another spec sale in 2006. An in-demand scriptcoach and seminar and workshop leader, Snyder provides information for writers through his website, *www.blakesnyder.com*.

$22.95 · 270 PAGES · ORDER NUMBER 75RLS · ISBN: 1932907351

THE MYTH OF MWP

In a dark time, a light bringer came along, leading the curious and the frustrated to clarity and empowerment. It took the well-guarded secrets out of the hands of the few and made them available to all. It spread a spirit of openness and creative freedom, and built a storehouse of knowledge dedicated to the betterment of the arts.

The essence of the Michael Wiese Productions (MWP) is empowering people who have the burning desire to express themselves creatively. We help them realize their dreams by putting the tools in their hands. We demystify the sometimes secretive worlds of screenwriting, directing, acting, producing, film financing, and other media crafts.

By doing so, we hope to bring forth a realization of 'conscious media' which we define as being positively charged, emphasizing hope and affirming positive values like trust, cooperation, self-empowerment, freedom, and love. Grounded in the deep roots of myth, it aims to be healing both for those who make the art and those who encounter it. It hopes to be transformative for people, opening doors to new possibilities and pulling back veils to reveal hidden worlds.

MWP has built a storehouse of knowledge unequaled in the world, for no other publisher has so many titles on the media arts. Please visit www.mwp.com where you will find many free resources and a 25% discount on our books. Sign up and become part of the wider creative community!

Onward and upward,

Michael Wiese
Publisher/Filmmaker